Leadership in the American Revolution

Library of Congress
Symposia on the American Revolution

Leadership
in the
American
Revolution

Papers presented at the third symposium, May 9 and 10, 1974

Library of Congress   Washington   1974

LIBRARY OF CONGRESS CATALOGING IN PUBLICATION DATA

Library of Congress Symposia on the American
    Revolution, 3d, 1974.
    Leadership in the American Revolution.

    1. United States—History—Revolution, 1775–1783—
Congresses. I. United States. Library of Congress.
II. Title.
E204.L53   1974   973.3   74-30110
ISBN 0-8444-0149-8

Advisory Committee
on the Library of Congress
American Revolution Bicentennial Program

John R. Alden
James B. Duke Professor of History, Duke University

Julian P. Boyd
Editor of The Papers of Thomas Jefferson, *Princeton University*

Lyman H. Butterfield
Editor of The Adams Papers, *Massachusetts Historical Society*

Jack P. Greene
Professor of History, The Johns Hopkins University

Merrill Jensen
Vilas Research Professor of History, University of Wisconsin

Cecelia M. Kenyon
Charles N. Clark Professor of Government, Smith College

Aubrey C. Land
Research Professor of History, University of Georgia

Edmund S. Morgan
Sterling Professor of History, Yale University

Richard B. Morris
Gouverneur Morris Professor of History, Emeritus, Columbia University

George C. Rogers, Jr.
Yates Snowden Professor of American History, University of South Carolina

Introduction

This symposium, entitled "Leadership in the American Revolution," is the third in a series of five Library of Congress symposia on the American Revolution that are being made possible by a grant from The Morris and Gwendolyn Cafritz Foundation. We are very grateful to the foundation for enabling the Library to present discussions of various aspects of the Revolution.

When I learned that it was to be my pleasure to present to you the presiding officer for this third symposium, Lyman H. Butterfield, editor in chief of *The Adams Papers,* my thoughts went back to a ceremony held when the first volumes of those papers were published. I was present on that occasion and wrote an account of it for the Library of Congress *Information Bulletin.* A rereading of that account, after more than a decade, led me to conclude that some parts of it were particularly relevant today. It began:

Vibrant with a family's sense of history and its sense of responsibility to the Nation, a ceremony at the Massachusetts Historical Society on Friday afternoon, September 22, 1961, marked the publication of the first four volumes of *The Adams Papers,* containing the diary and autobiography of John Adams.

Thomas Boylston Adams, president of the MHS, who presided, expressed his pleasure that the Adamses—who did not make it a habit to achieve popularity in their lifetimes—were at last attaining it, and his conviction that a working knowledge of history is essential to survival. "The fool and the rascal," he said, "have it all their way when the people do not have access to the sources."

Lyman H. Butterfield, editor-in-chief of the monumental undertaking to publish portions of the papers of the Adams family, which Edward Everett Hale called a "manuscript history of America," took a "brief bow." He called attention to the emblem devised for John Quincy Adams, which is used as the decorative motif for *The Adams Papers.* Consisting of an acorn and oak leaves, it bears a Latin inscription meaning "He plants trees for the benefit of future generations"; this symbolizes both the dedication of the Adamses to the service of their country and the importance of their papers for the continuing exploration of the American past.

Julian P. Boyd, editor of *The Papers of Thomas Jefferson,* spoke for the editors of the several projects within the program of the National Historical Publications Commission.

Terming Mr. Butterfield "an editor's editor," Mr. Boyd reminded the audience that the publication of such papers is not of importance to historical scholarship alone but, because of the discussion of American political institutions that was taking place then and is taking place now, it has "meaning for us as citizens."

The principal address of the day, entitled "The Adams Family and Their Manuscripts," was by the late Samuel Flagg Bemis. Permitted to use the papers before they were opened for research, he recalled that they were "handed out" to him from the inner sanctum. One reason they were not opened sooner, he said, was that the family provided its own historians and themselves worked with the papers. Henry Adams II was the last to serve as curator. He used to become so absorbed in the papers that he would talk to them, or to himself. "Confound it!" Professor Bemis would hear from the search room. "Abigail shouldn't have said that!"—an observation that might be applied to current situations.

On October 3, 1961, *The Adams Papers* were also honored in the Nation's Capital, where they were featured at a *Washington Post* book and author luncheon. Julian Boyd, Tom Adams, and Lyman Butterfield were again heard—in generous praise and modest disclaimer. Then the President of the United States, John F. Kennedy, rose. (He was later to review these first four volumes for the *American Historical Review*—surely a unique honor.) "I want to say to Mr. Adams," he began, "that it is a pleasure to live in your family's old house, and we hope that you will come by and see us."

For the day's extraordinary convocation he found three explanations.

First, he said, "Some of us think it wise to associate as much as possible with historians and cultivate their goodwill, though we always have the remedy which Winston Churchill once suggested in the House of Commons, when he prophesied during World War II that history would deal gently with us. And then in an afterword he [Churchill] said, 'because I intend to write it.' "

Second, "because all of us as Americans are constantly bemused and astounded by this extraordinary golden age in our history which produced so many men of exceptional talent. I have not heard, nor I suppose is there a rational explanation for the fact that this small country, possessed of a very limited population, living under harsh circumstances, produced so many, many, many brilliant and extraordinary figures who set the tone of our national life and who really represent the most extraordinary outpouring of human ability devoted to government, really, than any time since the days of Greece. And any touch which we may have in our lives with that period attracts us all."

Third, "because of our regard for the extraordinary record of the Adams family." He had "no doubt that Lyman Butterfield and Thomas Adams are breathing heavy sighs of relief—four volumes out, and only eighty or a hundred more to go. Obviously," the President said, "the worst is over."

And he concluded: "I congratulate all those gentlemen who have labored so long to produce these volumes. I congratulate Dr. Boyd who was a pioneer in this field. I congratulate those Presidents of the United States who in recent days have been most concerned that effective, contemporary records be kept. I congratulate us—I congratulate this country—I congratulate us all—in being part of the legacy which President John Adams left to us."

The proceedings, for all of us who shared in them, were memorable, and the words spoken, portentous.

Ladies and gentlemen, biographical details about the editor of *The Adams Papers* are readily available [see page 2]. It is my pleasure, at long last, to present the man whose work occasioned the tributes I've described—my dear friend and your fellow scholar, Lyman Butterfield, who will preside over this symposium.

ELIZABETH HAMER KEGAN
Assistant Librarian of Congress

Contents

vii
Introduction

3
Opening Remarks
L. H. BUTTERFIELD

7
American Political Leadership:
The Optimistic Ethical World View
and the Jeffersonian Synthesis
ALFRED H. KELLY

41
Congressional Leadership
in the American Revolution
MARCUS CUNLIFFE

63
The Democratization of Mind
in the American Revolution
GORDON S. WOOD

91
Military Leadership
in the American Revolution
DON HIGGINBOTHAM

113
Leadership in the American Revolution:
The Psychological Dimension
BRUCE MAZLISH

Leadership in the American Revolution

LYMAN H. BUTTERFIELD, editor of *The Adams Papers* at the Massachusetts Historical Society, graduated from Harvard University in 1930, began teaching there in the same year, and received his master's degree in English in 1934. He later taught English, American literature, and American history at Franklin and Marshall College and the College of William and Mary. He has held a lectureship in history at Harvard and an adjunct professorship in history at Boston University and is currently consulting editor on American history at Harvard University Press.

From 1946 to 1951 Mr. Butterfield served as associate editor of *The Papers of Thomas Jefferson* at Princeton University. During the following four years he directed the Institute of Early American History and Culture at Williamsburg, Va., before becoming editor of *The Adams Papers*. He is honorary consultant in American history to the Library of Congress and is a member of the Library's Advisory Committee on the American Revolution Bicentennial Program, of the board of editors of the *New England Quarterly*, the board of directors of the Council on Library Resources, and the Harry S. Truman Library Institute. He holds honorary degrees from Franklin and Marshall College, Bucknell University, and Washington College.

In addition to his editorial work on the Jefferson and Adams enterprises, Mr. Butterfield is author of *John Witherspoon Comes to America* (1953) and editor of a two-volume edition of *Letters of Benjamin Rush* (1951).

Opening Remarks

L. H. BUTTERFIELD

THE TOPIC of the third annual Library of Congress symposium marking the Bicentennial of the Nation's birth is leadership in the American Revolution. The subject is a timely and important one, in itself and in its implications both for Americans now experiencing a grave crisis in national leadership and, to employ a favorite phrase of the Founding Fathers, for "generations yet unborn."

Everyone is familiar with the article in our national faith holding that great crises produce great leaders. "When a society gets disturbed," John Adams wrote in 1780, "men of great abilities and good talents are always found or made." Actually this was a rather casual remark by Adams, who sensed more clearly than most of his contemporaries that the American Republic had not been exempted from the evils inherent in all institutions created and administered by fallible men. Nor was he speaking specifically of the United States. But the notion is older than history and widely prevalent in world folklore, as witness the idea of a saving prophet or divinity among the North American Indians, from the Hiawatha legend to the recent happenings at Wounded Knee.

Those speakers who touch on this belief in the papers that follow reach no common conclusion. But they agree with each other and with a long line of predecessors that the generation from 1763 to 1789 possessed remarkable capacities and talents. In an earlier paper in this Bicentennial series, Professor Henry Steele Commager observantly noted that European commentators were startled to find that Americans were electing their philosophers their kings, or at any rate their governors (and then mischievously added that it would be a good practice to revive). With the examples of Franklin, Adams, and Jefferson to support it, this is an assertion not easily denied.

But was the Continental Congress at any time, was the Federal Convention during its four months of deliberations, "an assembly of demigods" or "a Consistory of Kings"? If so—and this is a much more testing question—has the transit from Carpenters' Hall in 1774 to Watergate in 1974 been downhill all the way? If there are some disposed to answer yes, we may raise a further question: Are they not victims of a childish romanticism about the past and an equally groundless cynicism about the present? The two attitudes, as everyone knows, go readily hand in hand. And if this is too simple an interpretation of two centuries of national history, can we possibly discern a pattern of peaks and valleys, crests and troughs, in the evolution of our political leadership that would enable the increasingly skillful quantifiers among us to project their graphs into the future and, as it were, by using historical data find some assurance for us beyond history?

These are questions at or even beyond the frontiers of our discipline that concern us all, not only as historians but as citizens of the Republic. They not only engage our minds but touch our hearts. Few among us can be so scientifically dispassionate as to hold that there is no such thing as just national pride. For if there is not, there can be no just indignation and response when the Republic sustains injury at the hands of either leaders or followers.

Whatever the difficulties, no more appropriate time could be found to deal with these questions than now. And no more appropriate place could serve as a forum than the Library of Congress. Speakers in these symposia have rightly and repeatedly observed that our history as a nation is unique in the fullness of its documentation. In the 1830's and 1840's, while poets lamented the want of "old, unhappy, far-off things" to stir romantic feelings in America, antiquarians replied that, as one of them put it, if we had no "ivy-covered towers of ancient days," we had something better, "the prouder memorials of the Fathers of the Republic." In the gathering, preservation, and dissemination of these materials, the Library of Congress has for three-quarters of a century been in the forefront. For four of the towering figures in the generation of 1763–89—Washington, Jefferson, Madison, and Hamilton—it possesses the principal collections, and for a fifth—Franklin—one of the major collections. While it held custody of the Papers of the Continental Congress, the physical survival of which makes a story well warranting national pride, the Library published the *Journals* of that body, the best single guide we have to the events of 1774–89. In preparation for the approaching Bicentennial anniversaries, it began years ago a program, parts of which are near completion, to furnish in a single massive volume bibliographical guidance to the entire primary and secondary literature relating to the era of the American Revolution and to publish a series of particular guides to its own holdings in manuscripts, maps, and prints. It has launched an editorial project that will vastly enlarge and improve the familiar, invaluable, but fragmentary edition by Edmund C. Burnett of the *Letters of Members of the Continental Congress*. The conducting of these enterprises reflects leadership in the scholarly world of the most farsighted and indisputable kind, for which generations of historians "yet unborn" will be duly grateful.

This symposium begins on the very day the Judiciary Committee of the United States House of Representatives begins its hearings on impeachment of the President. The large attendance and the close attention to the scholarly proceedings at the Library manifests the wide and lively public interest in problems of leadership in our earliest history as a nation, no doubt sharpened rather than blunted by the constitutional proceedings nearby on Capitol Hill. Whatever the outcome, it is surely safe to venture the opinion that the qualities of leadership so admired in the American Revolutionary generation are capable of occasional self-renewal and, what is more, wholly in accordance with the forms prescribed by that generation.

The fabric of America has been woven of so many strands, its regions and cultures have been—and stubbornly remain—so disparate, and the ideas and ideals Americans have generated have been so numerous and clashing, that he who would generalize about any aspect of our national experience must be intrepid indeed.

Take American political leadership. What generalization can be broad enough to comprehend Governor Winthrop and Benjamin Franklin, Patrick Henry and Thomas Hutchinson, James Madison and Martin Van Buren, James G. Blaine and Grover Cleveland, William Jennings Bryan, the La Follettes of Wisconsin, Dwight D. Eisenhower, and the Kennedys of Massachusetts? And still say something more incisive than that this display adds up to more than a riotous diversity of individual talents and achievements, not unmixed, of course, with failures?

Professor Alfred H. Kelly of Wayne State University, one of our first authorities on the constitutional history of the United States, has intrepidly undertaken to trace a pattern in this luxuriant growth—to explain how American leaders embody and reflect the chief aspirations of their countrymen. Borrowing a phrase from Albert Schweitzer, he finds that American leaders typically express "an optimistic ethical world view." To be sure, the belief that the rewards of this world are rightfully theirs who righteously seek them has prevailed throughout western civilization since the waning of the Middle Ages. But Professor Kelly is right in pointing out that it has been a fundamental article in the American creed from the outset. In Philadelphia on July 4th, 1776, for the first time, the pursuit of happiness (captivating idea, captivatingly expressed!) was linked with life and liberty as an inalienable right of all citizens.

American Political Leadership
The Optimistic Ethical World View and the Jeffersonian Synthesis

ALFRED H. KELLY

FOR THE PURPOSE OF THIS PAPER, leadership will be defined somewhat arbitrarily as that combination of characteristics in a public figure which enables him to play an influential role in the life of the state. Put differently, a leader is one who commands an effective following for the formulation and implementation of public policy. In an open constitutional democracy the persons who perform this function are called politicians, although their immediate role may be that of President, governor, cabinet officer, Congressman, or Supreme Court justice. If very successful—and above all if they have succeeded to some extent in incorporating their ideas in the myths which impart vitality to the body politic—they will, after death, as the hoary witticism has it, be known as statesmen.

Quite evidently there are certain constants involved in political leadership in all ages and all conditions of man. These include, depending upon immediate circumstances, courage, the ability to inspire other men to action, the capacity to formulate those myths that give the social order vitality and supply it with a sense of legitimacy, the ability to manipulate the symbol system of the society effectively, and so on. The historian must on occasion recognize these qualities and deal with them, but their analysis is the peculiar province of the sociologist and psychologist, who have subjected them to extended treatment.

Quite aside from these constants, however, there are immense variations in the characteristics of political leadership as between societies, arising out of differences in such areas as geographic environment, historical heritage, economic system, institutional structure, and prevailing myth pattern. These differences are the peculiar province of the historian. He is quite aware that political leadership in the modern western world will upon examination be found to differ widely from that which existed in the ancient temple city-states of the Nile and Euphrates valleys, in a Greek polis of the Athenian era, or in a 13th-century Tartar horseback empire. Because he recognizes that American civilization has been and remains a part of the West, he may expect to discover in American political leadership many historical currents, ideas, institutions, and patterns of belief similar to those exhibited in the history of Britain or France. But Arnold Toynbee to the contrary, he knows also that American society and hence American political leadership will, upon examination, yield up certain factors which are peculiarly American.

It is not easy to set down those basic features of American society which have given American political leadership its special character. Quite simply, difficulties arise because—from one point of view at least—there has been not one American social order but many, separated widely in both time and space. They have ranged from the quasi-theocratic Massachusetts Commonwealth of John Winthrop, to the cotton slave plantation economy of the Gulf coastal plain in which W. L. Yancey once flourished, to the burgeoning Pennsylvania industrial economy which sent Thaddeus Stevens and "Pig Iron" Kelley to Congress in the 1860's, to the immensely complex urban industrial order with its pluralistic system of culture and economic and political power which provided the backdrop for the political careers of a Franklin Roosevelt, a John F. Kennedy, a Lyndon Johnson, an Adlai Stevenson, or a Richard Nixon. Yet certain constants are there.

Albert Schweitzer in his *Civilization and Ethics*[1] has characterized western civilization generally since the 17th century as exhibiting what he called an "optimistic ethical world view." Thereby he distinguished it sharply from the great generality of past nonwestern societies, which he described as "pessimistic ethical," because the latter, although they endowed life with moral significance, denied implicitly or even explicitly any solution to the tragedy of human existence other than final extinction. Schweitzer also distinguished modern western civilization from its earlier western Christian antecedents. The earlier West, he pointed out, posed a solution to the problem of human existence in terms of the next world; this life Jesus, Augustine, and Aquinas all found in its final essence to be utterly tragic. In the last two or three centuries, on the other hand, the modern West has committed itself to a solution of the problem of human existence in terms of this world.

The optimistic ethical view of reality, which Reinhold Niebuhr has pointed out constitutes a peculiar form of secularized Christian theological heresy,[2] has been entertained in America to a degree approached nowhere else in the West. It is one thesis of this paper that it has exercised a profound impact upon American political leadership, indeed that interpreted broadly it may be the principal distinguishing characteristic of that leadership, in that it supplies a major element of continuity linking the 18th and 20th centuries.

Briefly the optimistic ethical view of reality as entertained by American society and as formulated in one fashion or another by successive generations of American political leaders has held that this life—above all, life in America—is both fundamentally good and endowed with a self-sustaining ethical significance. It has held also that human nature, far from being depraved, irrational, or irredeemable, is in fact rational, ethically oriented, and committed fundamentally to the good. Or where, as in the more conservative American political tradition, it has considered after Augustinian theory that man is indeed to some considerable degree selfish, irrational, and even wicked, it has asserted nonetheless that man is sufficiently rational and good that he can, through the supremacy of law and the practice of limited government, control his impulses to depravity.

The American optimistic ethical view has as a consequence entertained a profound faith in man's ability to attack and solve systematically both social problems and those which impinge upon society and the state from a hostile physical environment. It has been suspicious of formal philosophical systems but at the same time deeply committed to a pragmatic empiricism in its approach to the public problem-solving process. Indeed, its political leaders since the 18th century may be characterized generally as assuming that the basic purpose for which political power is held and exercised is the solution of the problems confronting organized society. And with very few exceptions it has assumed that the dynamics of social development depend far more upon an overarching harmony of interest than upon any reality of class conflict.

Beyond all this the American world view has been committed to a dual standard of political legitimacy for the state: both to the idea of the supremacy of law as reflecting ultimately certain eternal verities of right and justice, and to the idea of a democratic process which resolves the potential conflicting interests of organized society in terms of the welfare of the majority of mankind. Finally it has believed that the American order is progressing toward some far-off paradise of earthly perfection, as yet perceived, as in Paul's aphorism, only "through a glass darkly": a vision of a noble and magnificent novus ordo seclorum in which the ancient curse pronounced upon the descendants of Adam and Eve will at length be lifted from all mankind.

It may well be objected that the average urban political boss, Congressman from New York, governor of Illinois or California, or President of the United States has not been greatly concerned with any of these things but has concentrated instead on the pursuit of power, in large part as a means to the dividing up of the loaves and fishes incident to public office. The average politician, our political realist will argue with some justification, would not even recognize what the so-called optimistic ethical myth is all about, let alone be concerned with its operational consequences.

To this it may be replied in the first instance that Thomas Jefferson, James Madison, John Adams, Abraham Lincoln, Oliver Wendell Holmes, Woodrow Wilson, Louis Brandeis, Felix Frankfurter, Hugo Black, and Adlai Stevenson, although they used a variety of symbols and metaphors to describe the same general body of ideas, have known very well what the optimistic ethical myth was all about. It has been political leaders of this calibre who have formulated the great statements that have both contributed to and inspired the various facets of the world view upon which American society has so long depended for its insight into ultimate political and social reality.

Moreover, even the pragmatic practitioners of internal realpolitik—those of the school of James Farley, Matthew Quay, George Boutwell, Roscoe Conkling, or Everett Dirksen (the latter in a moment of almost legendary frankness conceded that he had only one political principle: pure expediency and opportunism)—have been successful in considerable part because they have understood intuitively the limits which the optimistic ethical political myth imposed upon them, both with respect to acceptable goals of public policy and their modus operandi. They have understood and accepted, at the very least, that traditional American definition of an honest politician: one who never breaks his promise to another politician. In the immortal words of Boss Richard Croker, they have understood the difference between honest graft and crooked graft. And even the downright grafters and thieves—men of the stripe of Orville Babcock, "Smiler" Colfax, W. W. Bristow, William Tweed, Albert B. Fall, and William Hale Thompson—have generally been at pains to maintain an image of themselves as proponents of the optimistic ethical myth.

Prominent exceptions are few in number. One notable instance occurred in the South in the two or three generations before the Civil War, when the compelling realities of the slave system with its implied denial of the assertions concerning the nature and destiny of man set forth in the Declaration of Independence and the prominence which that society of necessity assigned to implied and even open violence as a device for compelling order led to a substantial repudiation of the optimistic ethical view of reality. Out of this background John Taylor of Caroline developed a theory of society and the state reminiscent both of Thrasymachus' argument in the first book of Plato's *Republic* and of Hobbes' *Leviathan*, both of which are utterly at odds with an optimistic ethical view of reality.[3] And John C. Calhoun, who at first gave evidence of his commitment to the optimistic ethical view, at length repudiated it in favor of an inverted Marxist conception of society and the political process.[4]

Almost alone among prominent American politicians, Aaron Burr apparently rejected deliberately the optimistic ethical myth in favor of a demonic or conspiratorial view of society and politics. (Only half seriously, I would argue that Burr translated the view of man propagated by Jonathan Edwards, his grandfather, who for 30 years preached that man was steeped in irredeemable depravity, into an operational theory of politics.) It is possible also that Senator Joseph McCarthy ought to be included as a proponent of the demonic conspiratorial view. But McCarthy was a reflection as well as a proponent of a certain paranoid streak in the American social order which on two or three occasions has threatened to overwhelm the optimistic ethical view both of politics and of the state. In this light, McCarthy emerges not merely as an American Titus Oates—he was very nearly that—but also as the pathetic image of a social psychosis which victimized him even as he attempted to convert it to political advantage.[5]

A great variety of historical, economic, social, religious, and ethical forces were responsible for the rise of the optimistic ethical myth in western culture and for the peculiar success it has enjoyed in American politics. It is possible to touch upon them only briefly here. Christianity supplied the West in the first instance with a profoundly ethical view of the nature of reality, offering a Manichean-like dualistic explanation of good and evil and holding mankind—including kings, ministers, and politicians generally—to a sharp standard of personal relationship to God.

The Puritan Revolution, responsible for a great deal of the early American world outlook, further sharpened and intensified the personal relationship between man and God. It created in early Americans what David Riesman calls an inner-directed standard of ethics and personal moral responsibility,[6] which one can find on page after page of the diary of a Samuel Sewall[7] or a John Quincy Adams.[8]

The West also early developed a dynamic rather than a static sense of society, a product perhaps in some part of the economic revolution in Europe that began as early as the 12th century but was derived also in part from the Judeo-Christian myth, which conceived of the historical process not as stable but rather as one involving struggle, progress, crisis, and ultimate resolution.

The great economic boom which began in western Europe in the 16th century, spread to America in the 17th, and continued with scarcely a break into the 20th also made a powerful contribution to the American optimistic ethical myth. The "great four hundred year boom," as Walter Prescott Webb not long ago labeled it, suffused western culture and America in particular with a spirit of daring, enterprise, and adventurous imagination which inevitably affected political psychology.[9] The successive triumphs of the scientific revolution initiated by Copernicus, Galileo, Newton, Vesalius, Descartes, and their fellows had much the same psychological impact. American politicians, at least from the time of the Revolution, have been problem-solving oriented; they have assumed that the same kind of daring and constructive imagination which yielded scientific knowledge, a series of technological triumphs, and a constantly accelerating spiral of production could be applied also to solve the problems confronting the state and organized society. The Constitutional Convention of 1787 was in part the product of this point of view.

Economic dynamism also had consequences for the class system. In America in particular, class lines became less rigid, allowing movement of individuals from one category to another, generally upward. As a consequence, most men at most times assumed that the quality of material life was improving. As early as the 18th century, a fair number of political leaders in America emerged from dynamic economic backgrounds involving upward class mobility. John Adams, James Wilson, Patrick Henry, John Marshall, and Thomas Jefferson all could fairly be so characterized. One consequence of the Revolution undoubtedly was to shake up traditional class lines and in general to increase class fluidity. In the 19th and 20th centuries, a fluid class background became typical of most successful American politicians rather than the exception. Abraham Lincoln epitomizes for us the log-cabin-to-White House myth, but the same general upward mobility characterized the careers of Andrew Jackson, Martin Van Buren, Stephen A. Douglas, Henry Clay, and Thaddeus Stevens, and a little later James A. Garfield, Herbert Hoover, John W. Davis, Harry S.

Truman, Lyndon Johnson, and a host of others. The consequence has been that most successful politicians have been steeped in the optimistic view of reality.

Vast numbers of Americans were of course excluded at one time or another from the benefits of economic dynamism and class fluidity. Negroes, locked into a separate caste system either in slavery or in freedom, were excluded almost entirely from the process until far into the 20th century. The small farmers of late 17th-century Virginia, ruined by competition with slave labor and pushed onto pine-barren uplands away from access to markets, the "poor white trash" of the Gulf coastal plain a century later, the immigrant and native whites toiling 12 hours a day in the mills of Homestead and Gary, and the migrant "Okies" of the era of the Great Depression were all in one fashion or another the victims rather than the beneficiaries of economic change.

There is no intention here to enter into the rather difficult argument over whether social mobility or class rigidity and social injustice historically have constituted the ultimate reality of the American social order. The important point is to recognize that social and economic immobility, recurrent poverty, and class conflict, however grim, have had comparatively little impact upon the prevailing optimistic ethical view of American society and politics. Negro intellectuals such as David Walker[10] could bitterly attack the American myth, but it meant little. Blacks were excluded outright from any role in either myth-making or political leadership. Political leaders generated out of local or regional discontent often overreached themselves, as did Daniel Shays and the misguided Pennsylvania frontiersmen involved in the Whiskey Rebellion. Or like Eugene V. Debs, Daniel De Leon, Benjamin Gitlow, and the handful of fellow Marxists and anarchists at the turn of the 20th century, they moved within their own closed circle of political reality, almost never breaking into the political mainstream or affecting seriously the prevailing American world view.

There was of course a native American reformist rationalist perfectionist radicalism which became politically prominent in the antislavery crusade and which in a variety of subsequent political guises found expression later in the Populist, Progressive, and New Deal eras. But almost without exception, the political leaders generated by these movements, from Joshua Giddings and Ben Wade to William Jennings Bryan, Charles A. Lindbergh, Sr., and Harold Ickes, conceived of themselves as dedicated to rescuing the American view of reality, not to its destruction. And when they turned to outright irrationalist or quasi-rationalist demagoguery, as did Populists Tom Watson and Joe Bailey, or Huey Long a generation later, they did so also in terms of some kind of optimistic view of reality and an ethical vision of social justice, however crude or corrupt their immediate symbols and notions of political means might be.[11] In short, the optimistic ethical view nearly always swallowed up dissident reformist politicians who made it into the mainstream. In some fashion, like William Jennings Bryan they accommodated themselves to it, consciously or no.

The American physical environment relative to the world at large also contributed to the optimistic ethical strain in politics. By mid-18th century, the Indian menace had been removed to the frontier, where it no longer threatened the centers of colonial civilization. The frontier itself might be one "long blood-stained line," as Frederick Jackson Turner later characterized it,[12] but policies of savage inhumanity, applied on too many occasions to solve the aborigine problem, seldom touched the consciences of the politicians involved, presumably because "redskins" like blacks were for the most part excluded from the assumptions and myths that governed the society at large. Jefferson could speculate in his *Notes on Virginia* that the American Indian was potentially the equal of the white man (he made a contrary assumption for Negroes),[13] but no one so far as I know challenged at the time General Sherman's brutal aphorism that "the only good Indian is a dead Indian." And Washington, Jackson, Van Buren, and Grant on one occasion or another all treated the Red Man as little better than vermin. The few politicians—notably John Marshall[14] and John Quincy Adams[15]— who on occasion thought of Indians as human beings entitled to rights guaranteed by a reign of law had comparatively little influence on public policy. The terrible realities involved in the "solution" of the Indian problem before 1900 at no time shook the faith of the typical American in the optimistic ethical point of view.

The position of the United States relative to foreign nations and empires also contributed to the American view of political reality. The outcome of the Revolution itself—an event viewed by many Americans as providential in character and implying a special American destiny—left the United States freed of any serious rivals for the domination of the North American continent. Accelerating population growth and economic power steadily increased the imbalance of American continental power as against other western hemisphere states. For Jefferson, Jackson, Tyler, Clay, and Polk, the intimation of an American special destiny became the basis for a realpolitik in American expansionism which in two generations took the republic from the Mississippi to the Pacific Ocean and involved the conquest and annexation of a large portion of Mexico.

Nor was this kind of realpolitik in foreign policy allowed to interfere seriously with the optimistic ethical view of the American world role. Jefferson and his successors simply assumed that the American experiment was fraught with the greatest significance for the welfare of all mankind. Hence the welfare of the United States and the welfare of all peoples ultimately were identical. Any moral problem involved in the rather high-handed techniques that were on occasion employed—in the annexation of Louisiana, the Floridas, Texas, and the northern two-fifths of the Republic of Mexico, for example—simply disappeared. The conduct of foreign policy did not seriously affect the society's ethical conception of itself, except in the eyes of an occasional dissident politician—Lincoln in 1847, for example.[16]

Economic dynamism, class fluidity, and a favorable geographic and power position, although indispensable to the eventual survival of the optimistic ethical myth, were in a sense all background. More immediately essential to the emergence of the American myth and its effective application to political leadership was the development of a workable synthesis between three distinct political ideas—constitutionalism, Enlightenment rationalism, and democracy—each of which involved differing and to some extent antithetical views of society, the political process, and the nature of political leadership. The achievement of this synthesis was, one may argue, the decisive American contribution to the vitality of the optimistic ethical view of reality in the modern western world. It provided the American political order with a dual system of legitimacy, one based both upon the supremacy of law and upon the idea of majority interest. Many men contributed to the achievement of this synthesis. Above all, however, it was the work of Thomas Jefferson and his political heirs and assignees of the following two generations.

Constitutionalism, the idea of the power of the state and its instruments as limited and controlled by the force of law, was the earliest of these three concepts to appear on the American political scene. The idea that the English king was under the law, a proposition promulgated in the 13th century by Bracton and 200 years later by Fortescue, was already centuries old when the American colonies were founded. The protracted 17th-century struggle between Parliament and the Crown was to some extent a dispute over the applicability of this very idea to the British constitutional system. The idea passed to the first New England colonies with their Puritan progenitors, and it found specific expression, in part out of Calvinist compact theory, in the earliest New England covenant colonies.

Thereafter constitutionalism won increasing acceptance throughout the American colonies. The growing popularity of the great natural law theorists—Vattel, Pufendorf, Harrington, Sidney, Milton, Burlamaqui, and

above all John Locke—contributed to its increasing acceptance. So also did
the introduction of the writings of Sir Edward Coke, whose *Commentaries,*
with their emphasis upon the element of natural right and justice in the
common law, became a professional bible for the 18th-century American
legal profession. By the time of the Revolution, constitutionalism had won
almost universal acceptance among American political leaders—indeed the
early American Revolutionary argument against Britain was formulated
very largely in constitutionalist terms.

Constitutionalism was both ethical and rational in character, but in and
of itself it was hardly either optimistic or democratic. Above all it recognized the element of the eternal in the universe—the ancient Stoic notion
that there is a natural harmony of things which may well reflect the ultimate nature of God and which man may discover for himself through the
application of reason. By this view of things men do not properly make
law, they merely discover and formulate law. Such a view of reality, without more, is static rather than dynamic; it emphasizes order, continuity and
the eternal, not progress, growth, or development. In a fundamental sense
the idea of constitutionalism and the idea of progress and social change are
profoundly antithetical. How can the eternal and the immutable properly
be compromised? It is no accident that constitutional precedent has always
been a ready refuge and shelter for conservative political leaders, from
Fisher Ames to John W. Davis. It offers a large measure of psychic security
and an assurance of the eternal in a society whose watchword has been
economic and social dynamism.

Nor was early American constitutionalism particularly optimistic in its
view of the nature of man—an essential element in any philosophy com-
prehending either intelligent social change or a workable democratic
process. Most of the natural law writers were reasonably optimistic about
man's fundamental nature, Thomas Hobbes being the notable outstanding
exception. But early American constitutional thought had a powerful
Calvinistic strain which, more than mere neo-Stoicism, recognized the
darker side to human nature. From this point of view, which John Adams,
John Jay, and to some considerable extent even James Madison all recognized, the rule of law was a means of restraining and controlling human
selfishness and predatory tendencies and balancing out the corruptive element of power in human affairs, which if left to itself presumably would
plunge society into chaos and anarchy.[17]

Early colonial political leaders were nearly all conservative constitutionalists, profoundly ethical in their view of the political process but little concerned either with any notion of social dynamism or with any optimistic

view of man. John Winthrop, Thomas Hooker, John Endicott, and even Roger Williams were all magisterial constitutionalists who held themselves responsible to both God and the covenant, and through the covenant to the body politic. Their conception of a Zion in the wilderness was in a very limited sense optimistic, but as good Calvinists they accepted the traditional Augustinian pessimistic ethical view of the meaning of life and the corollary assumption of the ultimate impossibility of solving the human dilemma in earthly terms.[18]

The progressive secularization of life in the course of the 18th century altered the nature of political leadership in New England somewhat. As the vision of the city on the hill faded, political power passed increasingly into the hands of a mercantile elite and their lawyer associates. The growing prestige of the common law now promoted the rise of a cadre of professional common law lawyers, who already were demonstrating a superior capacity to manipulate the instruments and symbols of the state.[19]

Nevertheless, the new mercantile lawyer elite, typified by such men as Jonathan Belcher, Samuel Sewall, Peter Oliver, and a little later Thomas Hutchinson, all exhibited a quality of stern and conscientious magisterial constitutionalism, tinged not a little by a growing optimistic ethical view, as Enlightenment values gradually penetrated the old Puritan stronghold.

Conservative constitutionalism, withal of a somewhat different variety, also prevailed in the southern colonies. Here the rise of a powerful landholding aristocracy resulted in a wedding between the idea of responsible magistracy—in this instance to the king or proprietor—and the notion of political leadership as both a manifestation and an obligation of dominant status in the class system. It was this conception of elitist magistracy which presumably motivated Robert Carter, designated "king" by his contemporaries, and the second William Byrd of Westover, both of whom served variously for more than a generation in the late 17th and early 18th centuries as members of the burgesses, as speaker, and as member or president of the governor's council. Both were devotees of an elegant amateur gentility and noblesse oblige in public life, which political leaders in the South were to imitate with varying degrees of success for the next 200 years.[20]

In the middle colonies, above all in Pennsylvania, there was evidence of a powerful new optimistic ethical element in the political process. Here the growth of cultural pluralism gave rise to a new breed of politician: the man who practiced the art of governing as a technique of balancing and compromising competing economic, class, and cultural interests. The men who mastered this technique were in a sense America's first successful pragmatic politicians. They anticipated the modes of maintaining themselves in power that Martin Van Buren, Henry Clay, Stephen A. Douglas, and still later Franklin Roosevelt and Harry Truman would practice long afterward.

Prominent among Pennsylvania politicians of this kind was Benjamin Franklin, who for nearly 30 years served successfully as clerk and member of the Pennsylvania assembly. Franklin combined an intense problem-solving-oriented political pragmatism with a powerful optimistic ethical view of the social process, quite evidently derived in part from Enlightenment influence. His view of reality led him into one experiment after another in sociopolitical reform—first in city and provincial affairs and later in intercolonial government.[21] David Rittenhouse, astronomer, mathematician, and engineer, who during the Revolution was to serve as president of the Pennsylvania Council of Safety, as a member both of the assembly and of the War Board, and finally as state treasurer, shared Franklin's pragmatic optimistic ethical view.[22]

By the time of the Revolution both Enlightenment ideas about man and society and the practice of political democracy were making heavy inroads on the American politicosocial order. Enlightenment values, as well as classic constitutionalism, suffused the American Revolutionary argument, particularly in its later phases.

The Declaration of Independence was in itself an attempt at a synthesis involving the values of constitutionalism, the Enlightenment, and democratic idealism. Not merely did it present a traditional natural law and compact theory of the origins, nature, and limitations of the state, after Locke, Vattel, and Burlamaqui; it also carried strong overtones both of the ideas of the philosophes and of the new winds of political democracy sweeping the states. It began by setting forth the notion of the equality of all men in natural law—an idea radically at odds with the assumptions of magisterial constitutionalism. Equally important, it set forth the even more unprecedented idea that the end of government was not so much the protection of property or vested rights in a common law or Lockean sense but rather the happiness of the people at large.

The Declaration thus carried the first modern intimation of the "greater happiness principle" to which most western governments have since dedicated themselves. The indictment of the king which followed was in the large to the effect that he had ignored the happiness and welfare of the Americans and instead had treated the colonies, in Channing's words, as "a great plum pudding."[23] Behind all this lay, by implication, a whole series of Enlightenment values: that rational men properly could pursue happiness, that is, the general welfare, an objective to be rationally defined, and by further implication that the notion of a better society could and should become a deliberate objective of public policy. The implications of all this for the new spirit of democracy are obvious enough.[24]

However plausible was the Declaration's immediate synthesis between constitutionalism, the Enlightenment, and emergent democracy, the gap both in theory and in practice between the three systems of ideas was in certain respects profound. To some extent, classic constitutionalism and the Enlightenment view of reality were complementary to one another. Both proceeded in considerable part out of the same general matrix of 17th- and 18th-century ideas about the universe, man, and society. Both assumed that the universe was rational, ordered, and coherent; both assumed that it was best understood not in terms of magic or the supernatural but by means of natural law; both assumed that man was sufficiently rational to discover and analyze the nature of reality.

But whereas constitutionalism, particularly the American variety with its secularized Calvinistic background, recognized the somber side of human nature with its potential for selfishness and corruptibility, Enlightenment thinkers from Diderot and Voltaire through Condorcet insisted that man was by nature both rational and good. Immediate human institutions which defied reason and enthralled man might be corrupt, as Voltaire had insisted so savagely in *Candide,* but man's potential for education, for improvement, for recognition and acceptance of the good, and for perfectibility remained unimpaired.

This in turn led to other potential contradictions in theory. Enlightenment thought, making itself manifest in America in the ideas of Jefferson, Franklin, Madison, Paine, and others, obviously assumed that change, progress, and perfectibility were desirable social objectives. But constitutionalism, with its emphasis upon the eternal, delineated those principles of an ordered society which must remain immutable regardless of the degree to which certain "superficial" externals undergo alteration and change. Finally, whereas constitutionalism recognized the potential clash between power and class interests, Enlightenment thought tended to emphasize the doctrine of the harmony of interest—the notion that all rational and good men had a substantially similar interest in commonwealth, progress, and perfectibility, which on most occasions would control if not subdue political conflict over rival power interests.

Constitutionalism and emergent republican democracy, if not absolutely irreconcilable, were also profoundly at odds with one another. Again, constitutionalism posed as an ethical frame of reference the eternal and the immutable; democracy, by contrast, posed as a frame for legitimacy majority will and majority interest, which are most unlikely to have anything immutable about them. Further, constitutionalism declared certain values to be absolute, while democracy set up shifting popular will as a good. This last may not necessarily even be the same thing as public welfare, let alone have the quality of an eternal good. Jonathan Boucher, conservative American Tory who was intensely aware of the intimate relationship between the American Revolutionary spirit and democratic sentiment, pointed out all these contradictions and dilemmas very nicely at the time of the break with Britain.[25]

But the lifestream of politics, at least in the immediate sense, like that of the law, involves experience, not pure logic, and the threat these theoretical differences posed to the prospects of political commonwealth in the new republic were for a time concealed. The intensity of the quarrel between the colonies and Britain and the subsequent struggle for independence submerged for the most part—although certainly not entirely—the differences between political leaders of widely varying ideological backgrounds, class interests, and philosophies. It drove into momentary patriotic cooperation, for example, George Washington, heir to the magisterial constitutional tradition of the Virginia tidewater, and Tom Paine, an egalitarian reformist revolutionary.

Again, most political leaders and public figures who held to a traditional conservative constitutional view of the political process—the Peter Olivers, Thomas Hutchinsons, and Jonathan Bouchers—turned Tory. The common execration directed against them helped to create a temporary atmosphere of substantial political unity. Finally, all theory aside, most of the prominent leaders of the Revolutionary era were, without examining too deeply the logical difficulties involved, both constitutionalists and, in varying degrees, sons of the Enlightenment. This characterization could be applied fairly not merely to Thomas Jefferson, James Madison, Benjamin Franklin, John Dickinson, James Wilson, and Roger Sherman but also, to some extent, to George Washington, John Adams, Samuel Chase, Henry Laurens, John Rutledge, Charles Cotesworth Pinckney, and John Jay.

To a surprising degree this consensual situation carried over into the Confederation era and the 1787 Convention. In spite of the growing political dissent manifested during the latter Confederation era by debtors, dissident planters, and upland farmers, the Convention itself was overwhelmingly a consensual affair, so far as underlying constitutionalism and Enlightenment orientation were concerned. The sharp differences of policy and opinion which developed in the Convention between the nationalist and states' rights factions tended momentarily to disguise the fact that almost all the delegates, from George Washington, James Wilson, Gouverneur Morris, Rufus King, and C. C. Pinckney to James Madison, Roger Sherman, Oliver Ellsworth, George Mason, and Elbridge Gerry, were constitutional republicans who adhered also to Enlightenment values concerning man and society.[26]

The document these men produced thus was both a republican instrument and a creation of the Enlightenment. In its flexibility, in its combination of experimentalism and conservatism, and in the implied assumptions it embodied about man and society it was also a product of ethical optimism. This orientation is hardly surprising, for the delegates were essentially the same group of men—or their immediate political successors—that had adopted the Declaration 11 years earlier, although they were now functioning in a different capacity.[27] There were important underlying differences between the delegates in the theories of government and society which they entertained, but they did not manifest themselves significantly in the Convention.

These differences, long suppressed by the exigencies of Revolution and national constitutional crisis, broke into the open in the Washington and Adams administrations. The partisan quarrel between Federalists and Democratic-Republicans was admittedly in considerable part a conflict inspired by sectional, class, and economic differences. But it is important to recognize that the argument was also ideological and philosophical. It rested to a substantial degree upon cleavages having to do with the nature of society and the sociopolitical process, with constitutionalism, and with the nature and destiny of man. Put in terms of leadership, it was, conceived broadly, an argument between proponents of a magisterial conception of constitutionalism and those who proposed to derive political legitimacy from a nascent synthesis between constitutionalism and democracy. Closer examination yields three major ideological positions among politicians of the Federalist era: that of the constitutional conservatives or magisterial constitutionalists, that of the constitutional moderates, and that of the constitutional democrats.

Washington himself emerges upon analysis as almost a paradigm of magisterial constitutionalism of the later variety. Constitutionalism, now couched in a republican mold, for Washington meant security for property and religion, integrity in government, and harmony and order in organized society. Although his roots were Anglican and hardly Calvinist, he had comparatively little Enlightenment faith in man as a rational animal and apparently conceived of the new government above all as an instrument for obtaining that legitimacy for the exercise of political power which in Britain had arisen out of the sacrosanct status of monarchy, parliament, and the common law.

Washington's view of the French Revolution illustrates nicely his social and constitutional conservatism. In his letters to Lafayette he applauded the limitations which the National Assembly had placed upon a hitherto irresponsible monarch,[28] but at the same time he expressed to Lafayette and others the fear—all too justified in the event—that revolutionary reformism, severed from its traditional legitimism, might end by plunging France into violence, anarchy, and despotism. In like fashion, Washington's celebrated Farewell Address is almost a prescription for a golden age, based upon harmony, religion, morality, and political stability. Washington did approve of the idea of progress; in 1783, for example, he wrote:

> The foundation of our Empire was not laid in the gloomy age of Ignorance and Superstition, but at an Epocha when the rights of mankind were better understood and more clearly defined, than at any former period, the researches of the human mind, after social happiness, have been carried to a great extent, the Treasures of knowledge, acquired by the labours of Philosophers, Sages and Legislatures, through a long succession of years, are laid open for our use, and their collected wisdom may be happily applied in the Establishment of our forms of Government.[29]

But there is little evidence that the revered Virginian appreciated the significance of this situation in relation to his views upon the ultimate nature of leadership of the state, nor did he entertain any idea of any very special American destiny.

With the exception of Alexander Hamilton, other conservative Federalists, with some variations, shared Washington's belief in magisterial constitutionalism. John Jay, distinguished diplomat, Chief Justice of the United States, governor of New York, and author of five of the Federalist papers, in the course of his career exhibited a consistent nationalism, an extraordinary integrity, and a stubborn commitment to an aristocratic political style. Gouverneur Morris, brilliant in the Philadelphia Convention, thereafter demonstrated a consistent contempt for the masses, a feeling no doubt strengthened by his on-stage reaction to the excesses of the French Revolution after 1792. John Rutledge and C. C. Pinckney were planter aristocrats; their concern with slavery effectively inhibited any notion of social progress or any dream of destiny they might otherwise have entertained. Rufus King, convention delegate, diplomat, and United States Senator, showed comparatively little interest in any idea of democracy or Enlightenment-oriented reformism until the slavery controversy touched him in his old age.[30] And Fisher Ames, patriot and staunch magisterial constitutionalist, was again a man of great integrity and talent, but his contempt for any popular element in republicanism placed him closer to Tories Jonathan Boucher and Thomas Hutchinson than to even the moderate constitutionalists of his day. The world view of these men was ethical, and patriotic, and limned with integrity, but it was optimistic only in its hope for order and security if magisterial government were not disturbed by the mob.[31]

Alexander Hamilton, who was to make vast contributions to American constitutional theory, was nonetheless farther than any of the foregoing from any optimistic ethical point of view toward government, man, or society. His fears of Levellism and his contempt for the masses were classically conservative; his notion of the proper foundation of government was Hobbesian rather than magisterial, resting upon a theory of a concordance of selfish interests rather than any archaic notion of functional class harmony such as other Federalists entertained. More than most other conservatives, he recognized America's potential for economic dynamism, yet he failed almost entirely to recognize economic dynamism's meaning as a possible instrument for altering the social order. And he was so far from accepting any idea of consensual American community that in 1798 he apparently could hope that the Republicans would blunder into insurrectionary civil war and so be destroyed.[32] He was privately increasingly contemptuous of the Constitution itself, which in a letter of 1802 to Gouverneur Morris he described as a "frail and worthless fabric."[33] None of this should obscure the fact that Hamilton in his Bank Message and Pacificus papers made contributions of vital importance to the evolution of constitutional government in the United States. But he was in no sense an adherent of an optimistic ethical view of man or society—including American society.

In spite of the deep strain of conservatism in his political ideas, John Adams, with his ultimate faith in republican government, his partial recognition of the significance of the American experiment, and his partial vision of American progress, deserves to be classified as a constitutional republican. Adams' conservatism arose in the first instance out of his secularized Calvinism. He had deserted the Augustinian notion of total depravity, but he could not accept the theory that man was naturally good, and he was contemptuous of Diderot, d'Alembert, Condorcet, and the other philosophes with their easy assumptions of natural social harmony and human perfectibility. But unlike Hamilton, Fisher Ames, and the other High Federalist conservatives, Adams trusted aristocracy no more than he did the mass of men; both, he observed, had their demagogues, their rapacities, and their irrational passions. It was for this reason that he so admired the Constitution, which like Madison he read as balancing out competing class interests, thereby promoting the only kind of harmony and stability possible in this world. Nor did he confine his vision of progress to economic exploitation; instead he recognized its potential for a dimly perceived larger American destiny, which he found to be desirable and good.[34]

Far more in the mainstream of American constitutional development— in some respects even more so than Adams—was James Wilson, the Scottish immigrant boy who rose to prominence in Pennsylvania and the Continental and Confederation Congresses as a protege of John Dickinson. Wilson's immediate political ideas, as his biographer Charles Page Smith has pointed out, had very conservative roots, being derived by way of Richard Hooker from Thomas Aquinas and other medieval natural law theorists; as such they emphasized the element of immutability, harmony, order, and the eternal in law. Nor was Wilson any radical democrat in his immediate associates. A friend of the rich and powerful, he sought speculative wealth as frantically as the most exploitative-minded men of the hour.[35]

But Wilson, paradoxically enough, had within him the makings of a constitutional democrat. In the Philadelphia convention he emphasized repeatedly that constitutional government derives its just powers from the consent of the people. This led him to argue—unsuccessfully—for the direct election of Senators and, what is more surprising for his time, for the direct popular election of the President himself. Again, in his celebrated 1790 lectures on the common law, Wilson once more emphasized that the foundations of government lay in popular sovereignty, while he manifested also a powerful self-consciousness about the meaning of the American political experiment and the republic's destiny. America's future history, he declared, would one day eclipse that of "glorious Greece," because already it was "distinguished by a love of liberty and a love of law."[36] Wilson's immediate commitment to conservative politics, in short, has disguised the fact that he was far closer in his ideas to modern constitutional democracy than were any of his Federalist fellows.

It is difficult to know whether to classify James Madison as a constitutional moderate or a constitutional democrat, for the very simple reason that there were, in a manner of speaking, two Madisons. The Madison of 1787 was undoubtedly a constitutional moderate, committed strongly to the idea of the erection of a national government of adequate sovereignty and a relatively broad spectrum of delegated powers. And while unquestionably he was a son of the Enlightenment, with a concomitant faith in human reason, he showed no very extraordinary interest in popular democracy. The Federalist papers—above all his much celebrated no. 10—make clear once more his interest in constitutionalism as a device for balancing out class conflicts and for reconciling economic and social differences between the three principal geographic sections of the republic.

The Madison of 1798 had become a lieutenant of Thomas Jefferson. No longer was he interested primarily in national sovereignty, which he had some time since come to fear as a potential instrument of exploitative Hamiltonian capitalism. Instead, in the Virginia Resolutions he demonstrated himself to be primarily concerned with reemphasizing the sovereignty of the states which, with Jefferson, he apparently now considered the appropriate repositories for a political authority representative of an expansionist agrarian democracy. Still a constitutionalist and a believer in the reign of law, he had adopted a position on federal-state relations which made him, by one interpretation at least, Calhoun's spiritual father and the grandfather of the Civil War. The transformation was testimony to the compelling power of party politics and sectional interest, but not to any abandonment of either constitutionalism or the Enlightenment.[37]

It was Thomas Jefferson, Madison's political chief, who solved effectively the contradictions and inconsistencies between constitutionalism, the Enlightenment view of man, and political democracy, in such a way as to effect a workable synthesis of all three. The consequence was the emergence of new maturity in the American optimistic ethical approach to the political process. The result made possible a new American political community which restored the consensual situation in American politics which had prevailed in the Convention. A dual system of legitimacy now came into being. The state now drew its sanctions both from the Constitution and from popular will; each of these in turn depended upon an optimistic ethical view of man, society, and American destiny. Thereby Jefferson performed one of the greatest feats of political leadership in the entire sweep of American history.

Jefferson's first major accomplishment was the restoration and revival of the idea of a popular republican American political community, which had been nascent in the 1780's but which by 1800 had been in some danger of being lost entirely. He did this by projecting upon the body politic the notion of a common body of values, myths, ideals, and objectives about American society, to which all but a few reactionary High Federalists subscribed, regardless of immediate party affiliation. This idea he advanced prominently in his First Inaugural, with his celebrated aphorism that "We are all Republicans; we are all Federalists."

Thus Jefferson incorporated into contemporary American political thought and practice the idea of the harmony of interest, which has been with us ever since. It assumed that almost all members of the body politic had a sufficiently large stake in the preservation, welfare, and future of constitutional democracy to reconcile themselves to immediate differences between factions and sections and to accept with some grace failure to attain immediate selfish goals when political defeat made such attainment impossible. Winners and losers, in other words, ultimately shared common goals and a common destiny. Only a few reactionary extremists who refused to accept any such idea of community or any such assumption of destiny were to be thrust into the outer darkness.[38]

Jefferson coupled this theory of community with a new theory of democratic will which supplied constitutional government with a new frame of reference for republican legitimacy: the idea of the greatest good for the greatest number. It was a notion which Jeremy Bentham even then was engaged independently in refining as a theory of governmental ethics and which John Stuart Mill later was to categorize as utilitarianism. However, Jefferson's conception of the common good was more sophisticated and enlightened than Bentham's, at least in American terms, since it integrated the idea of the "greatest good" with the conception of minority rights, as a part of Jefferson's larger synthesis of constitutionalism, Enlightenment values, and democracy.[39]

Jefferson's idea of a democratic community and his "greatest good" test for the legitimacy of public policy solved the old conflict between traditional constitutionalism and the Enlightenment view of man, upon which Boucher, Fisher Ames, and other conservatives had dwelt. It equipped Jefferson and his party with a practical operating objective for political policy: the pursuit of the general public welfare. It was a body of theory and practice far more at home in the explosive dynamism of America's economy, population, and social order, what with their concomitants of class fluidity and upward mobility, than was magisterial Federalist constitutionalism or the Hobbesian expansionism of Hamilton. From this time forth, with one tragic exception, practically all mainstream American political leaders would be equipped with an optimistic ethical view of American society which assumed both constitutional supremacy and the capacity of the democratic political process to solve effectively the problems of a dynamic economy and social order.

Only in the South was the growing political problem of the defense of slavery to eventuate in a body of political leaders—Calhoun, Howell Cobb, Alexander H. Stephens, John Y. Mason, Robert Barnwell Rhett, and so on—who would turn away from the Enlightenment presumptions about the nature and destiny of man and finally even the idea of open constitutionalism itself in an effort to protect the "peculiar" southern labor system. The result was a backward-oriented dream that sought vainly to preserve an archaic order in an era of dynamic change.

For the rest of the country, Jefferson vastly invigorated the American dream. Jefferson, of course, did not originate the American sense of destiny. It had had its origins, in one sense at least, as far back as the Puritan vision of a new Zion. The leaders of the Revolution were intensely self-conscious about the significance of the break with Britain for the potential perfectibility of American society and the future of mankind at large.

But with Jefferson, the idea of a special and extraordinary American destiny, one associated presumably with the mission of the United States ultimately to bring constitutionalism, republicanism, and an open society to the world at large, became a dominant and self-conscious American political theme. The United States, Jefferson proclaimed in his First Inaugural, was "a rising nation . . . rapidly advancing to destinies beyond the reach of mortal eye." Thereafter, until well into the 20th century, a series of prominent American political leaders, among them Jackson, Polk, Webster, Lincoln, Wilson, and finally Franklin Roosevelt, with his "rendez-vous with destiny," adopted the idea of an extraordinary American destiny as a prominent part of their ideological baggage.

The Jeffersonian synthesis resolved to a very considerable extent the conflict of political leadership between conservative constitutionalists, constitutional moderates, and constitutional democrats. Conservative or magisterial constitutionalists in the paradigm of Hamilton, Fisher Ames, or Gouverneur Morris disappeared within less than a generation. Almost all of the succeeding two generations of political leaders claimed to be sons of Jefferson; as such they professed belief in constitutional democracy, progress, the harmony of interest, the idea of an American political community, and a special American destiny. In short, American political leaders now committed themselves to a mature optimistic ethical political myth. That myth was to survive far down into the 20th century; indeed, in spite of some considerable damage it remains alive today. Virtually all political leaders profess to subscribe to it. For a political leader openly to repudiate it would be to invite destruction.

However, the numerous practical politicians of the period between 1820 and 1860 developed one very important modification of the Jeffersonian idea of political community: the notion of political parties as a device for resolving economic, class, and sectional conflicts without breaking in too seriously upon the common sense of a harmony of interest. Jefferson had assumed that argument and discussion among enlightened and intelligent men would produce the truth without the necessity for political parties. The experience of the 1790's seemed to imply that parties were dangerous and even subversive institutions fearfully destructive of the idea of community and inimical to the process of Enlightenment-oriented political discussion. In the absence of any really adequate common body of political ideas to serve as a common point of departure in political debate this was probably true. But acceptance of the Jeffersonian synthesis opened up a new possibility.[40]

What Henry Clay, Martin Van Buren, Daniel Webster, William L. Marcy, Andrew Jackson, Thomas Hart Benton, Lewis Cass, James K. Polk, Stephen A. Douglas, and the innumerable lesser lights that revolved around them in the political firmament discovered was a mode of applying the common-law system of advocacy to political disputes. It is no accident, I think, that virtually all the political leaders of the middle period of American history were trained professional lawyers. They had been schooled in the ancient common-law idea that the presentation in a case of opposing arguments neither of which in itself embodies anything like the whole truth leads somehow to a final resolution of a dispute in terms of something like truth and justice.

The political leaders of the middle period simply transferred this system of advocacy to the realm of politics. Common-law-type advocacy now became institutionalized in a new system of political parties, within which political leaders functioned in an intensely practical fashion, bargaining and arguing over sectional, political, and economic interests, but without disturbing too seriously the overall sense of community involved in the general acceptance of the optimistic ethical point of view. The great majority of politicians, with the partial exception of those from the South, played the game according to a set of rules which involved a common body of assumptions about the Constitution, American society, the political process, and American destiny. The supremacy of law, the validity of republican government, and the democratic political process, the idea of nationhood, the harmony of interest, and the sense of American destiny all were taken for granted.

Politicians from opposing political parties, with varying economic interests, and from differing sections of the country often were personal friends in private life—witness the warm personal relationship between Martin Van Buren and Henry Clay. Even Abraham Lincoln and Alexander H. Stephens for a time maintained something of a friendship of this kind; indeed, Stephens appealed to his recollection of Lincoln's integrity and decency in the Georgia secessionist convention as an argument against taking the state out of the Union.[41]

It was the slavery controversy, of course, which momentarily broke this political community down. In the immediate sense this happened because the stakes of the game between the sections had become too high to make it possible to preserve any longer the idea of any real harmony of interest between North and South. But if one peers a little deeper, it becomes apparent that southern politicians some time since had abandoned the optimistic ethical view of reality. They did so, one may argue, to throw the necessary psychic shelter around their "peculiar institution." By the time of the Missouri Compromise they had already abandoned the affirmation of equality and natural rights set forth in the Declaration of Independence. Not long after that Calhoun also abandoned the idea of the harmony of interest in social structure in favor of his inverted proto-Marxist conception of the class struggle. From this point of view, the institution of slavery first broke down the optimistic ethical myth in the South; this in turn led to a failure of the idea of community with the rest of the nation, throughout which Enlightenment ideas of natural right and the perfectibility of man were very much alive. The result was a profound psychic rupture between North and South, symbolized by William H. Seward's appeal to the idea of a "higher law" and Calhoun's attempt to invoke the notion of a "concurrent majority"—a virtual abandonment of the American community in favor of a republican "dual monarchy."[42]

Meanwhile in a somewhat different political arena, that of the Supreme Court, a not altogether different group of practical lawyer-politicians, headed first by John Marshall and then by Roger B. Taney, was incorporating an optimistic ethical national myth into constitutional law. At first any such similarity between the ideas of Jefferson and those of Marshall appears to be absurd. Marshall's principal accomplishment, every elementary text assures us accurately enough, was to translate Hamiltonian political ideas into constitutional doctrine. But while Marshall's debt to Hamilton is obvious, the great Chief Justice was far more than a Hamiltonian shadow. Marshall made his own immense contribution: the idea of a republic based upon the supremacy of law and founded also upon the reality of an American community moving forward to an expansive destiny. Americans, he assured the legal audience which waited upon him, were for many purposes one sovereign people. The Constitution was no mere statute; instead it was meant to endure for ages to come. It was to be construed not in any narrow immediate sense but in the interests of future generations of

Americans. Nor was Marshall, concerned as he was with vested rights, interested in property as an end in itself; instead, he saw property as an essential instrument in the maintenance of community. In short, Marshall, no friend of his cousin Jefferson, deliberately participated in the prevailing sense of national community and national destiny. In a profound sense, Marshall's constitutional law was optimistic ethical in its view of American society and the American nation.[43] With the exception of his tragic Dred Scott opinion, Taney adopted essentially the same view of American reality.

With Jefferson, Marshall, and the party politicians of the two generations before the Civil War the political formulation of the American optimistic ethical myth was essentially complete. Thereafter it exhibited a tremendous vitality, which carried it almost unimpaired far into the 20th century. Thus Lincoln continually invoked the Jeffersonian synthesis and the Marshallism concept of nationhood to give vitality to the Union cause in the Civil War. The war itself he envisaged as a tremendous crisis of a nation committed to a synthesis of constitutionalism and democracy; the great question at issue was "whether a nation so conceived and so dedicated" could "long endure." The Gettysburg Address is, in its entirety, a magnificent piece of blank verse dedicated to the optimistic ethical view of the American nation, its special destiny, and its meaning for mankind at large. And the war itself, begun in gloom and uncertainty, obviously became a reformist crusade, confined within sharp limits by a powerful constitutionalist tradition.

The Jeffersonian synthesis between constitutionalism and Enlightenment-oriented reformist democracy also dominated the so-called Radicals of the Reconstruction era. In a fundamental sense the argument between Andrew Johnson and the Republican Radicals was a dispute over whether a decidedly conservative and static view of the constitutional process and state-federal relations or a progressive rationalist reformist view both of the constitutional process and southern reconstruction should prevail. But it is a great mistake to view the Republican Radicals as breaking outside the confines of the constitutional system as Marshall had defined it. On the contrary, Thaddeus Stevens, Benjamin Wade, Charles Sumner, John A. Bingham, Lyman Trumbull, and Henry Wilson, all of whom were powerfully motivated rational reformists, were also confirmed constitutionalists, as needless to say were the more pragmatically oriented Republican Radicals: James G. Blaine, Roscoe Conkling, Benjamin Butler, John A. Logan, Oliver P. Morton, John Sherman, Zachariah Chandler, George Boutwell, William Pitt Fessenden, and Simon Cameron. The refusal to abandon constitutionalism was in fact one of the major reasons for the comparative failure of Radical congressional reconstruction. From this point of view, the congressional Radicals were in fact not radicals at all; they were instead far inside the Jeffersonian optimistic ethical synthesis.[44]

The optimistic ethical view of political reality as synthesized by Jefferson and formulated in nationalistic terms by John Marshall quite evidently has lasted far into the 20th century. Politicians of the last 70 years of American history have almost without exception operated within the optimistic ethical view of reality. From one point of view at least, they can be seen as falling at various points along a spectrum ranging from the conservative constitutionalists to the rationalist reformers who have attempted to implement a latter-day Enlightenment-motivated conception of the perfectibility of man. Henry Cabot Lodge, Herbert Hoover, William Howard Taft, James A. Reed, John W. Davis, Henry L. Stimson, Carter Glass, Alfred E. Smith, and Cordell Hull, while they differed vastly in immediate social and economic background and party affiliation, were all in the final analysis constitutional conservatives concerned above all with preserving precedent, order, and continuity in the political system. Significantly, however, every one of them also exhibited, in a variety of ways and in varying degrees, a problem-solving orientation toward the political process, while on occasion they also devoted important portions of their careers to rationalistic reformism.

At the other end of the political spectrum have been the reformer idealists, most of them in terms of 20th-century realities directing their energies toward eliminating what they have conceived to be the corruptive impact of monopoly capitalism upon the American dream. The list is long and impressive: it includes George W. Norris, Theodore Roosevelt, Louis D. Brandeis, Charles A. Lindbergh, Sr., Robert La Follette, Harold Ickes, Henry A. Wallace, William E. Borah, Hiram Johnson, Harlan F. Stone, Harry Hopkins, Newton D. Baker, Wendell Willkie, and above all Woodrow Wilson and Franklin D. Roosevelt. Significantly, almost every one of these men was a lawyer, all exhibited some considerable concern for constitutional supremacy, and nearly all were pragmatic political practitioners who, in the tradition of the party politicians of the 1830's and 1840's, bargained and maneuvered for position and power.

Brandeis, Wilson, and F.D.R., in particular, are testimony to the vitality of the optimistic ethical political synthesis. Brandeis, after amassing a small private fortune, thereafter devoted his entire life to the purification of the American socioeconomic-political order and to the notion of an American industrial commonwealth conceived almost entirely in Jeffersonian terms.[45]

Wilson first attempted a reform of the American order largely in Jeffersonian terms, then plunged into a tragic attempt to impose upon the world at large an international institutional structure reflecting almost completely the Jeffersonian optimistic ethical synthesis.[46] F.D.R., opportunist, empiricist, experimentalist, and cunning practitioner of pragmatic politics, was in the final analysis a firm adherent of the optimist ethical view of reality: a constitutionalist, a rationalistic reformer, and even a utopian who flirted now and again with the Wilsonian view of world order.[47]

Today the American optimistic ethical view of reality is in deep trouble. The difficulty begins with the very foundations of the myth itself, where most of the assumptions involved in the original Jeffersonian synthesis are under serious attack. The Enlightenment view of man as a being both rational and fundamentally good has been badly damaged; in place of the optimism of the Encyclopedists we have the systematic portrayal by psychologists from Freud and Watson to B. F. Skinner of man's inability to make rational decisions based upon genuine free will. Worse yet, the advertising and public relations industries have converted the rational theories of man's irrationalism into a highly effective operational technology damning to the notion of a Jeffersonian community making enlightened free choices in the arena of public policy.

The ethical foundations both of constitutionalism and of democracy also have been badly damaged. The ancient Judeo-Christian conception of reality, with its view of life as ethically meaningful in a larger sense and staged within a universe significant for man, which the Enlightenment secularized, has been replaced to a considerable extent with a view of the universe as ethically meaningless and devoid of any process of resolution. The notion of a natural harmony in the universe discoverable by human reason—the ancient foundations of natural law and natural right—is also almost abandoned. David Hume dealt natural law its first terrible blow, and today only a few theorists such as Leo Strauss and certain neo-Thomists have persisted in the idea.[48] The consequence is that constitutional law has lost most of its original logical foundation as the explication of immutable truths about man's nature and destiny, natural law and natural right.

The idea of a Jeffersonian political community based upon an overarching harmony of interest also has suffered severely. One special-interest group after another—labor leaders, capitalists, black militants, student radicals, and so on—has assumed that what it conceived to be the unjust imbalance of power in the social order, the difficulty of achieving social change through traditional legitimate political channels, and the crying need for the immediate rectification of grievous injustice or grave social wrong has justified the resort to "direct action," which generally has meant the invocation of violence, either actual or implied. The result has been severe damage to the idea of a political community where social change supposedly was to be accomplished only through the political process and through alteration in the law.

Participation by the United States in an international state system in which the idea of community as propounded by Grotius and Vattel has been nearly extinguished has also had unhappy repercussions for the internal political community. It was only a little more than 40 years ago that Henry L. Stimson observed, as he closed down the State Department's code-breaking office, that "gentlemen do not read each other's mail."[49] Or to put the matter differently, the United States stood for an ethic in the international as well as in the internal order, which the secretary of state did not intend to betray. But our political leaders in charge of foreign affairs have, so to speak, been "reading each other's mail" for some time now.

Of late, the techniques of amoral Machiavellian realpolitik which we have come to accept, reluctantly perhaps, as somehow necessary for the conduct of foreign policy, have "leaked over" into the conduct of internal political policy. The consequence is that Republican and Democratic politicians, or some of them at least, have begun to treat each other with the same tender regard that secret agents of the Soviet Union and the United States exhibit for one another in the international community. One consequence of all this has been the loss of the spirit of Eden-like innocence that once characterized our optimistic ethical world view. Many Americans now exhibit a deep pessimism about our own political integrity and about the ethical validity of America's role, both in world affairs and in internal policy.

In turn this has meant a loss by the American political community of its sense of special destiny. Most Americans now believe that we are not going anywhere in particular; St. Paul's darkened glass is now clouded over completely. The last hint of a Wilsonian mission in the world, set forth in all sincerity by Dean Rusk and Walt Rostow, was extinguished in the swamps and jungles of Vietnam. At best we now hope to solve the energy crisis, preserve our standard of living, and avert the holocaust of a doomsday bomb.

It would be an error to suppose that all this has been fatally destructive of American political leadership cast in the optimistic ethical style, but the consequences are nonetheless painfully apparent. Almost every President of the United States, from Franklin Roosevelt to Richard Nixon, has been "caught out" in a direct lie, a political style, if we may so dignify it, that is difficult to associate with the integrity of a Washington, an Adams, a Lincoln, or even a Calvin Coolidge. The entourage of most Presidents of late has included the wheeler-dealer operator who peddles and trades influence backstairs: Lamar Caudle, Sherman Adams, Bobby Baker, H. R. Haldeman, and John D. Erlichman. Presidents, Theodore White assures us, are no longer the products of a public political process; instead, they are manufactured or "made" by public relations experts, an operation costing scores of millions of dollars.[50]

Certain political leaders for some time now have come to treat prominent members of the opposition party as the enemy, thereby junking the concept of a common political community as an outworn notion. To this end they have engaged in illicit wiretapping, mounted internal spying operations startlingly like those conducted by the CIA abroad, violated the restrictions of the Fourth Amendment, planted false and libelous stories about political opponents, and even indulged themselves in political burglary, withal in a somewhat clumsy and amateurish fashion. Much of this sort of thing, incidentally, began well before the present administration took office; in fact, it might be argued that the incidence of political skullduggery has been growing geometrically in the last generation.

Yet the optimistic ethical myth and its close concomitant the optimistic ethical style of political leadership are far from dead in America. Within the last two decades or so Estes Kefauver, Adlai Stevenson, Hubert Humphrey, George McGovern, John F. Kennedy, and—with some limitations— Lyndon Johnson have shown themselves to be, with varying degrees of sophistication and success, rationalistic reformists in the Enlightenment perfectionist Jeffersonian tradition. The Supreme Court, made up of men recruited from both major political parties, has in the person of William O. Douglas, Earl Warren, Hugo Black, William Brennan, and Thurgood Marshall devoted itself to an Enlightenment-oriented perfectionist reformism, although it has sometimes engaged in decidedly peculiar historical mythmaking to support its conclusions. Nor have constitutional conservatives limned with integrity and sensitive to the Enlightenment view of man been absent from the scene. John Marshall Harlan, Barry Goldwater, Felix Frankfurter, Nelson Rockefeller, Sam Ervin, and Warren Burger all have demonstrated their devotion to this tradition. There are many others.

In short, we are witnessing today the enactment of an ancient historical drama: the ebb and flow of conflicting values and of the men who champion them as part of a grand process of struggle, conflict, and potential resolution. The process, it may be observed, is profoundly western, and even more profoundly American. For the moment crisis is too much with us; our vision is darkened and the future obscured. Those of us who long ago subscribed to the classic American view of reality will, of necessity if for no other reason, continue to envision the grand panorama of American history in optimistic ethical terms. But whether we are witness to a Shakespearean-type tragedy, a protracted episode involving struggle and resolution in the style of Beethoven's Ninth Symphony, or merely a light skit staged in a Theater of the Absurd none of us here is likely ever to know.

Notes

[1] Albert Schweitzer, *Civilization and Ethics,* trans. C. T. Campion, 2d ed. (London: A. & C. Black, 1929), pp. 11–31.

[2] Reinhold Niebuhr, *The Irony of American History* (New York: Scribner, 1952); see also the argument in Reinhold Niebuhr and Alan Heimert, *A Nation So Conceived: Reflections on the History of America From Its Early Visions to Its Present Power* (New York: Scribner, 1963).

[3] John Taylor was in his immediate stance a republican constitutionalist but his view of human nature and of nearly all social order was Hobbesian. See, for example, the argument in his *Construction Construed, and Constitutions Vindicated* (Richmond: Printed by Shepherd & Pollard, 1820), pp. 10–17, where he observed that "almost all governments have espoused and nourished the spirit of avarice . . . and have betrayed the weak, whom it was their duty to protect." In *Inquiry Into the Principles and Policy of the Government of the United States* (Fredericksburg, Va.: Green and Cady, 1814), pp. 12, 13, 28, 31, 36, he assured the reader in effect that aristocracy in origin was founded on "religious frauds" and derived its authority from "the sanctity of oracles . . . and the holiness of priests," now "the scoff of common sense." Democracy, he added, like monarchy and aristocracy, is ultimately founded upon man's propensity "to do good to himself . . . [and] evil to others" (ibid., p. 76). The argument that almost all government rests on "force and fraud" occurs again in Taylor's *Tyranny Unmasked* (Washington: Davis and Force, 1822), pp. 17–18, 58.

[4] On Calhoun's proto-Marxist elucidation of the class struggle as inherent in the American social and political system, see his "South Carolina Exposition and Protest," in *The Works of John C. Calhoun,* ed. R. K. Crallé, 6 vols. (New York: D. Appleton and Company, 1851–56), 6:24–25, 36–37. See also the interpretations in Richard N. Current's *John C. Calhoun* (New York: Washington Square Press, 1966) and "John C. Calhoun, the Marx of the Master Class," in *The American Political Tradition and the Men Who Made It* by Richard Hofstadter (New York: A. A. Knopf, 1948).

[5] Robert Griffith, *The Politics of Fear: Joseph R. McCarthy and the Senate* (Lexington: Published for the Organization of American Historians by the University Press of Kentucky, 1970); Richard Hofstadter, *The Paranoid Style in American Politics, and Other Essays* (New York: A. A. Knopf, 1965).

[6] David Riesman, *The Lonely Crowd; a Study of the Changing American Character* (New Haven: Yale University Press, 1950).

[7] Sewall's diary entry of February 15, 1677, is typical of many such: hence he prayed that God might take away his pride and let him "be content with God's wisdom: though it might seem to uncovenanted reason [to be] foolishness." *The Diary of Samuel Sewall, 1674–1729*, ed. M. Halsey Thomas, vol. 1 (New York: Farrar, Straus and Giroux, 1973), pp. 35–36.

[8] In his entry of July 11, 1796, for example, Adams observed: "I enter this day upon my thirtieth year. The periodical days of reflection are seldom satisfactory to me. The principal reproach my conscience can make me, for the last year, is too much time spent in relaxation, perhaps lost. Let me strive to make a better improvement of the next." *Memoirs of John Quincy Adams, Comprising Portions of His Diary from 1795 to 1848*, ed. Charles F. Adams, vol. 1 (Philadelphia: J. B. Lippincott & Co., 1874), pp. 172–73.

[9] In *The Great Frontier* (Austin: University of Texas Press, 1964), pp. 13–28 ff., Walter Prescott Webb sets forth his "boom theory" of western culture.

[10] *David Walker's Appeal, in Four Articles, Together With a Preamble, to the Coloured Citizens of the World, but in Particular, and Very Expressly, to Those of the United States of America*, ed. Charles M. Wiltse (New York: Hill and Wang, 1965).

[11] See, for example, C. Vann Woodward, *Tom Watson: Agrarian Rebel* (New York: Macmillan Co., 1938), and T. Harry Williams, *Huey Long* (New York: A. A. Knopf, 1969). In Williams' work Long emerges not merely as a demagogue but in part also as a man motivated genuinely by an ideal of social welfare.

[12] Frederick Jackson Turner, *The Frontier in American History* (New York: H. Holt and Co., 1920), p. 45.

[13] In his *Notes on the State of Virginia*, ed. William Peden (Chapel Hill: Published for the Institute of Early American History and Culture, Williamsburg, Va., by the University of North Carolina Press, 1955), pp. 139–43, Jefferson compares and contrasts the cultural potential of Indians and blacks.

[14] In *Cherokee Nation v. Georgia*, 5 Peters 1 (1831) and *Worcester v. Georgia*, 6 Peters 515 (1832), Marshall asserted that Indians had certain rights under the Constitution which both the states and the federal government were bound to respect.

[15] E.g., Adams' attempt to protect the Creek Indians in the possession of their lands against the incursion of Georgia's Governor Troup. See *A Compilation of the Messages and Papers of the Presidents, 1789–1897*, by James D. Richardson, vol. 2 (Washington: Government Printing Office, 1896), pp. 370–73. Adams in 1841 called United States Indian policy "among the heinous sins of this nation, for which I believe God will one day bring them to judgment...." John Quincy Adams, *Memoirs*, 10:491–92, quoted also in Lynn H. Parsons, " 'A Perpetual Harrow Upon My Feelings': John Quincy Adams and the American Indian," *New England Quarterly* 46 (September 1973): 339–79.

16 On the occasion of his celebrated "Spot Resolution," *Congressional Globe,* 30th Congress, 1st Session, December 22, 1847 (Washington: Printed at the Globe office for the editors . . . , 1848), p. 64; also in Abraham Lincoln, *The Collected Works of Abraham Lincoln,* ed. Roy P. Basler, 9 vols. (New Brunswick, N.J.: Rutgers University Press, 1953), 1:420–22.

17 Most notably by Madison in his celebrated Federalist paper no. 10. See Benjamin F. Wright, ed., *The Federalist* (Cambridge: Belknap Press of Harvard University Press, 1961), pp. 129–36.

18 See Morgan's excellent introductory essay in Edmund S. Morgan, ed., *Puritan Political Ideas, 1558–1794* (Indianapolis: Bobbs-Merrill, 1965), and Perry Miller's *Orthodoxy in Massachusetts, 1630–1650* (Cambridge: Harvard University Press, 1933).

19 Perry Miller, *The New England Mind: From Colony to Province* (Cambridge: Harvard University Press, 1953). See also Thomas J. Wertenbaker, *The Puritan Oligarchy; the Founding of American Civilization* (New York: C. Scribner's Sons, 1947).

20 Louis B. Wright, *The First Gentlemen of Virginia* (Charlottesville: University Press of Virginia, 1964), pp. 235–85; 312–47.

21 Paul W. Conner, *Poor Richard's Politicks: Benjamin Franklin and His New American Order* (New York: Oxford University Press, 1965).

22 Edward Ford, *David Rittenhouse, Astronomer-Patriot, 1732–1796* (Philadelphia: University of Pennsylvania Press, 1946).

23 Edward Channing, *A History of the United States,* vol. 3, *The American Revolution, 1761–1789* (New York: Macmillan Co., 1927), p. 81.

24 Richard Buel, "Democracy and the American Revolution: A Frame of Reference," *William and Mary Quarterly,* 3d ser. 21 (April 1964):165–90.

25 Jonathan Boucher, *A View of the Causes and Consequences of the American Revolution; in Thirteen Discourses, Preached in North America Between the Years 1763 and 1775* (London: Printed for G. G. & J. Robinson, 1797); see also Anne Y. Zimmer and Alfred H. Kelly, "Jonathan Boucher: Constitutional Conservative," *Journal of American History* 58 (March 1972): 897–922.

26 On the Convention as essentially a consensual gathering see Leonard W. Levy, "Making the Constitution," in his *Judgments: Essays on American Constitutional History* (Chicago: Quadrangle Books, 1972), pp. 5–15.

27 For a contrary view of the matter see Stanley Elkins and Eric L. McKitrick, "The Founding Fathers; Young Men of the Revolution," *Political Science Quarterly* 76 (June 1961): 181–216.

28 Washington to Lafayette, August 11, 1790; Washington to Lafayette, July 28, 1791, in *The Writings of George Washington,* ed. John C. Fitzpatrick, 39 vols. (Washington: U.S. Government Printing Office, 1931–44), 31:85, 362. Washington to Gouverneur Morris, October 13, 1789, ibid., 30:442. On July 28, 1791, Washington wrote directly to Lafayette expressing sympathetic concern at the "disorders and incertitude" in France; the "indiscriminate violence" of the "tumultous populace of large cities" was "ever to be dreaded." Ibid., 31:324.

[29] Ibid., 26:485.

[30] Robert Ernst, *Rufus King, American Federalist* (Chapel Hill: Published for the Institute of Early American History and Culture at Williamsburg, Va., by the University of North Carolina Press, 1968).

[31] On the ideas of Fisher Ames and like-minded conservatives, see David H. Fischer, "The Myth of the Essex Junto," *William and Mary Quarterly*, 3d ser. 21 (April 1964): 191–235.

[32] Stephen Kurtz, *The Presidency of John Adams; the Collapse of Federalism, 1795–1800* (Philadelphia: University of Pennsylvania Press, 1957), pp. 314 ff. See also John C. Miller, *Alexander Hamilton: Portrait in Paradox* (New York: Harper, 1959).

[33] Hamilton to Gouverneur Morris, February 27, 1802, in *The Works of Alexander Hamilton,* ed. Henry Cabot Lodge, 9 vols. (New York: G. P. Putnam's Sons, 1885–86), 8:591–92.

[34] Adams' political ideas are set forth at length in *A Defence of the Constitutions of Government of the United States of America* (London, Printed, Boston, Re-printed and sold by Edmund Freeman, 1778). See also Zoltan Haraszti, *John Adams & the Prophets of Progress* (Cambridge: Harvard University Press, 1952), which is based principally upon the marginal notes Adams penned in his books.

[35] Charles Page Smith, *James Wilson: Founding Father, 1742–1798* (Chapel Hill: Published for the Institute of Early American History and Culture at Williamsburg, Va., by the University of North Carolina Press, 1956), pp. 309–41.

[36] James Wilson, *The Works of James Wilson,* ed. James D. Andrews, vol. 1 (Chicago: Callaghan and Co., 1896), pp. 1–3.

[37] Madison's continuing devotion to both constitutionalism and democracy becomes apparent in Adrienne Koch's *Jefferson and Madison; the Great Collaboration* (New York: A. A. Knopf, 1950). See also *Power, Morals, and the Founding Fathers; Essays in the Interpretation of the American Enlightenment* (Ithaca, N.Y.: Great Seal Books, 1961); and the essay on Madison in Richard B. Morris' *Seven Who Shaped Our Destiny; the Founding Fathers as Revolutionaries* (New York: Harper & Row, 1973).

[38] *The Jeffersonian Tradition in American Democracy,* by Charles M. Wiltse (1935; reprint ed., New York: Hill and Wang, 1960), is the best brief exposition of Jefferson's political theories relative to constitutionalism, democracy, and the Enlightenment.

[39] The "test of morality" for Jefferson, Gilbert Chinard concluded, was "general interest and social utility." *Thomas Jefferson; the Apostle of Americanism* (Ann Arbor: University of Michigan Press, 1957), p. 525.

[40] In *The Idea of a Party System; the Rise of Legitimate Opposition in the United States, 1780–1840* (Berkeley: University of California Press, 1969), Richard Hofstadter analyzes the post-Jeffersonian conception of the role of parties in the political process.

[41] American Historical Association, *Annual Report* (Washington, 1911), vol. 2, p. 487. Lincoln, in correspondence with Stephens on the eve of Georgia's secession, alluded to their former friendship. Lincoln to Stephens, December 22, 1860, in Lincoln, *Collected Works,* 4:160. See also James G. Randall, *Lincoln, the President; Springfield to Gettysburg,* vol. 1 (New York: Dodd, Mead & Co., 1945), p. 219.

[42] See Benjamin F. Wright, "The Southern Political Tradition," in William H. Nelson, ed., *Theory and Practice in American Politics* (Chicago: Published for William Marsh Rice University by the University of Chicago Press, 1964), pp. 83–100.

[43] Especially pertinent are Marshall's words in *McCulloch v. Maryland,* 4 Wheaton 316 (1819), and *Gibbons v. Ogden,* 9 Wheaton 1 (1824). Leonard Baker, in *John Marshall: A Life in Law* (New York: Macmillan Co., 1974), emphasizes the democratic theme in Marshall's career, beginning with his role in the Virginia ratifying convention of 1788. In *The Jurisprudence of John Marshall* (Princeton, N.J.: Princeton University Press, 1968), Robert K. Faulkner emphasizes that Marshall viewed property not as an end but as a means to the construction of community.

[44] See Alfred H. Kelly, "Comment on Harold Hyman's Paper," in Harold M. Hyman, ed., *New Frontiers of the American Reconstruction* (Urbana: University of Illinois Press, 1966), pp. 40–58.

[45] Brandeis' correspondence illustrates dramatically his devotion to rationalistic reformism under law. Melvin I. Urofsky and David M. Levy, *Letters of Louis D. Brandeis,* 3 vols. (Albany: University of New York Press, 1971–73).

[46] The transition in Wilson's career is sketched effectively by Harley Notter in *The Origins of the Foreign Policy of Woodrow Wilson* (Baltimore: Johns Hopkins Press, 1937). For Wilson's internal reform program see Arthur Link, *Wilson,* vol. 2, *The New Freedom* (Princeton, N.J.: Princeton University Press, 1956).

[47] See the interpretation of F.D.R. as a political tactician in James McGregor Burns' *Roosevelt: The Lion and the Fox* (New York: Harcourt, Brace, 1956).

[48] Leo Strauss, *Natural Right and History* (Chicago: University of Chicago Press, 1953).

[49] Quoted in Allen Dulles, *The Craft of Intelligence* (New York: Harper & Row, 1963), p. 71.

[50] Theodore H. White, *The Making of the President, 1968* (New York: Atheneum Publishers, 1969).

Vice chairman of the Detroit Bicentennial Commission, chairman of the Wayne State University Bicentennial Commission, parliamentarian of the American Historical Association, and a member of the Permanent Committee for the Oliver Wendell Holmes Devise of the Library of Congress, Alfred H. Kelley is professor of history at Wayne State University. He was codirector for research and drafting at the Michigan Constitutional Convention, 1961–62.

Professor Kelly, who holds Ph.B. (1931), M.A. (1934), and Ph.D. (1938) degrees from the University of Chicago, began his teaching career as an instructor at Wayne University in 1935 and was made assistant professor in 1940. Following a leave of absence for military service, 1944–46, he returned to Wayne University as associate professor. He was appointed chairman of the Department of History in 1952.

Professor Kelly's publications include *The American Constitution: Its Origins and Development* (with W. A. Harbison, 1948, 1955, 1963, 1970), *Foundations of Freedom* (1958), and *American Foreign Policy and American Democracy* (1954).

A few days after what only later became known as the First Continental Congress convened, John Adams wrote: "There is in the Congress a collection of the greatest men upon the continent, in point of abilities, virtues, and fortunes." But six weeks later he revised his opinion: "In Congress, nibbling and quibbling—as usual. . . . These great wits, these subtle critics, these refined geniuses, these learned lawyers, are so fond of showing their parts as to make their consultations very tedious."

Adams loved hyperbole. But at one time or another most of the delegates, or at least those whose thoughts are at all fully on record, expressed the same contradictory views. And so, according to their predilections, historians have been able ever since to characterize the "old Congress" (or Congresses) as the noblest body of legislators since Cicero addressed his fellow senators in Rome, or as a company of self-important provincials who, after July 1776 at any rate, spent their time mostly in squabbling with each other while Washington and his French allies won the war.

The issue is far from settled today among serious students of the American Revolution. Professor Marcus Cunliffe of the University of Sussex addresses himself to the large and complex problem of why this is so. A British scholar deeply versed in American cultural and institutional history, the author of several books distinguished alike for learning and readability, Professor Cunliffe asks more questions than he provides answers for, and furnishes many more suggestions than hard conclusions. But his questions are searching, and his suggestions open pathways that will certainly, and soon, be well traveled.

Congressional Leadership
in the American Revolution

MARCUS CUNLIFFE

JOHN ADAMS FEARED THAT undue credit would be given to the military leaders in the American Revolution, at the expense of the civilian patriots. In the popular imagination, Adams predicted, the importance of Benjamin Franklin would also be much overrated. "The history of our Revolution," he grumbled, "will be one continued lie from one end to the other. The essence of the whole will be that Dr. Franklin's electrical rod smote the earth and out sprung General Washington. That Franklin electrised him with his rod, and thenceforward these two conducted all the policy negotiation, legislation, and war." Looking back as an old man on what had happened, Adams still worried that the record had not been put straight, and that it never would be. "Who," Adams wondered in a letter to his friend-enemy Thomas Jefferson in 1815, "shall write the history of the American revolution? Who can write it? Who will ever be able to write it? The most essential documents, the debates and deliberations in Congress from 1774 to 1783, were all in secret, and are now lost forever." Jefferson replied in the same vein. "On the subject of the history of the American revolution, you ask who shall write it? ... Nobody; except merely its external facts. All its councils, designs and discussions, having been conducted by Congress with closed doors, and no member, so far as I know, having even made notes of them, these, which are the life and soul of history, must for ever be unknown."[1]

The first thing to be said about this exchange is that both men appear to assume that what went on in the Continental Congress during the first decade of its existence is the key to the history of the Revolution. Another observation most people might agree with is that posterity has borne out some of Adams' misgivings. The acts and opinions of the Continental Congress are much more abundantly documented than Adams or Jefferson could have realized. A great deal has survived in the way of private correspondence and memoirs, together with the fairly full Journals of Congress maintained by its permanent secretary Charles Thomson. Historians have plenty to chew upon. Yet far more has been written about Washington and his generals, their tribulations and triumphs, than on the parallel efforts of Congress. True, the fundamental issues of republican democracy which so much exercised Adams and Jefferson and their contemporaries have been closely analyzed. A recent distinguished example is Gordon Wood's book *The Creation of the American Republic*.[2] But I think it fair to say that in many of these analyses one gains the impression that, intellectually speaking, the Founding Fathers disappeared into a tunnel after the Declaration of Independence and did not really stick their heads up again until the latter part of the 1780's.

My paper is concerned with the "councils, designs and discussions" of the era Adams and Jefferson had in view, that is, from 1774 to 1783. Having for some time been curious about the operations of the Continental Congress, in a rather idle and unsystematic fashion, I welcomed the opportunity provided by this symposium to do some thinking on the problem. I must confess that I have not got very far. Indeed I may be more confused than before I started. I cling to the consolation that confusion is inherent in the subject. All scholars will, I fancy, be familiar with what we may call the chameleon effect—the tendency to take on the lineaments of one's chosen field. If you study Henry James your prose style becomes an unwitting parody of his. If you immerse yourself in Edmund C. Burnett's edition of the *Letters of Members of the Continental Congress* you are apt, to judge from my experience, to fall into the collective mindset of the delegates.[3] This phenomenon is characterized by a kind of cosmic parochialism, or highminded peevishness—and caused to a considerable extent, I think, by a sheer ineradicable semantic mixup. It is often extraordinarily hard to tell what may have been meant by such words as *nation, confederation,* and *strength*. In certain cases the delegates made confusion worse confounded by inability to express themselves lucidly. Sometimes— this is where the cosmic parochialism comes in—they used high-sounding arguments to dignify or disguise a piece of special pleading on behalf of their state or some other client. But often they were the victims of an extraordinary ambiguity in the terms they were obliged to employ.

In fact, I am tempted to speculate whether, in stressing the dearth of materials, Adams and Jefferson may not have concealed from themselves the deeper reasons why no one by 1815 had produced a history of the Continental Congress. They were right in remarking that the survivors of the Revolution were not impeccable witnesses; Jefferson himself misremembered the exact timetable of the signing of the Declaration of Independence. But the human memory is notoriously unreliable, and documentary evidence may likewise be suspect. Through the span of history these recognized limitations have not deterred participants or scholars from constructing their versions of the truth. Adams, after all, had many of the instincts of an archivist. He and Jefferson, during or after the event, wrote quite copiously about episodes in their careers. They must have known that Thomson, the secretary of Congress, kept official journals from 1777 and may have expected him to have preserved unofficial ones before that date. They may have been unaware that in 1783 John Jay had urged Thomson to write the political history of the Revolution—a theme, said Jay, "most liable to misrepresentation"—for which he was the ideal author. Two years later Thomson told François de Barbé-Marbois, the French consul-general, that he was well along with the task. He had already, he claimed, compiled more than a thousand folio pages—"secret historical memoirs of everything which has not been inserted in the public journals"—that would "complete the history of the revolution." In actuality Thomson seems never to have put together more than a bare beginning— a few pages labeled "History of the Confederation." He may have had personal reasons, such as jadedness or subsequent understandable pique when he lost his job at the expiry of the Continental Congress in 1789 and was not even invited to President Washington's inauguration. But he lived on until 1824, as Adams and Jefferson did know, and was alert enough in retirement to produce a four-volume translation of the Bible. He can hardly have supposed that his projected history would be unreadably dull. My suggestion is that he, Adams, and Jefferson sensed that the topic was unwriteably complex, not mainly because its issues were still controversial but rather because they continued to elude definition.[4]

This semantic slipperiness can be illustrated from a post-Revolutionary clash between Edmund Pendleton and Patrick Henry, who had both served in the First Continental Congress of 1774–75. The occasion was the Virginia convention summoned in 1788 to consider ratifying the new federal Constitution. Pendleton favored ratification; Henry opposed it. In order to back up his position, Pendleton reviewed the role of the federal government during the War of Independence. "Not . . . Confederation," he maintained, "but common danger, and the spirit of America, were bonds of our Union: Union and unanimity, and not that insignificant paper, carried us through that dangerous war. 'United, we stand—divided, we fall!' echoed and re-echoed through America—from Congress to the drunken carpenter—was effectual. . . ." The "insignificant paper" was of course the Articles of Confederation. Pendleton continued: "This spirit had nearly reached the end of its power when relieved by peace. It was the spirit of America, and not the Confederation, that carried us through the war. Thus I prove it: the moment of peace showed the imbecility of the Federal Government. . . ." Pendleton was referring in particular to the failure of the Continental Congress to resolve the issue of the nation's debts. Patrick Henry rejected Pendleton's interpretation. "The Confederation," said Henry, "this same despised government, merits, in my opinion, the highest encomium. It carried us through a long and dangerous war; it rendered us victorious in that bloody conflict with a powerful nation; it has secured us a territory greater than any European monarch possesses; and shall a government which has been thus strong and vigorous, be accused of imbecility, and abandoned for want of energy?"

On the face of it there is nothing remarkable about this clash; it is simply a "nationalist" and an "anti-Federalist" squaring off against one another. The intriguing feature is that each man uses the arguments we might have expected the other to adopt. Pendleton comes close to saying that America should introduce a more energetic form of central government, in the shape of the 1787 Constitution, because in wartime the Confederation had been carried along by the "spirit of America"—which must mean the popular will. Henry's case for the Articles, on the other hand, comes close to saying that America should retain a weak central government because in wartime it had proved itself anything but weak. Pendleton disparages the apparatus of government: Henry specifically congratulates the government, not the nation as a whole, for being "strong and vigorous."[5]

Apparent ambiguities and reversals of logic of this sort are characteristic of the period. The obvious difficulty is that Congress took upon itself several of the functions of a sovereign government: declaring war, declaring independence, directing the war effort, regulating finance, borrowing money, making treaties of commerce and alliance, establishing the central instrument named the Articles of Confederation, forming a policy for the settlement and incorporation of western territories, negotiating peace terms, and so on. Yet in the first decade of its existence a majority of the delegates at any given time probably mistrusted everything that words like strength and vigor connote when applied to central government. Some believed Congress should remain in being only for the duration of the emergency. So the demand was for a government both modest and efficient, both ideologically pure and realistically successful. The semantic snags, my main concern for the moment, were considerable. In what vocabulary could one either praise or blame a government thus limited and yet expected to accomplish great things? A possible solution, which has some weight of historical evidence in its favor, is to take the Pendletonian line in an anti-Federalist sense. Thus, one could contend that Congress was responsible only in a general, rhetorical sense; the term *Congress* or *Confederation* was merely a convenient shorthand reference to the American people or to the 13 sovereign states.

Possibly so, but then a more generous rule is applied to commanders of armies, whose control may likewise be remote and indirect. Since they are blamed when battles are lost, they are allowed to take the credit when battles are won. Alexander Hamilton sounds more consistent than Pendleton or Henry in a pamphlet of 1783 in which he implies that Congress resembles a general with insufficient resources:

It is . . . painful to hear, as is too fashionable a practice, indiscriminate censure heaped upon Congress for every public failure and misfortune, without considering the entire disproportion between the means which that body have it in their power to employ, and their responsibility. . . . The good deeds of Congress die, or go off the stage with the individuals who are the authors of them, but their mistakes are the inheritance of those who succeed. . . .

Congress stand in a very delicate and embarrassing situation. On the one hand, they are blamed for not doing what they have no means of doing; on the other their attempts are branded with the imputations of a spirit of encroachment, and a lust of power.[6]

But if Hamilton's logic is impressive, his motives can be discredited. Are we left with a choice between men who offered bad arguments for good reasons and those who offered good arguments for bad reasons?

And does the concept of "leadership" help us or get us into even more of a semantic mess? There are several different kinds of leadership. There is the sort equated with force of character. There is a managerial type, closely related to the ability to organize. There is the leadership that comes from the ability to put ideas into clear form and memorable language, either on paper or in speech. There is moral leadership, in which the life-style of the leader is of a nature to inspire admiration and emulation. There is a symbolic leadership, in which a person or a group epitomizes the aspirations of the community. There is also perhaps a manipulative leadership exerted by people who possess wealth or influence. The men who were elected to Congress were nearly all leaders in one or more of these categories, having already made some mark for themselves in their own states. The only exception to this statement is that some may have been chosen as *potentially* suitable, or as stand-ins for more powerful figures who could count on them to follow instruction. The letters written by delegates provide a continual mutual assessment. Three complaints frequently recur. The first is that the standard of Congress has declined. For example, the New Jersey delegate Abraham Clark wrote on July 4, 1776: "I am among a Consistory of Kings.... I assure you Sir, Our Congress is an August Assembly, and can they Support the Declaration now on the Anvil, they will be the greatest Assembly on Earth." By 1783, however, former delegate Benjamin Rush of Pennsylvania could write that "the Congress is abused, laughed at and cursed in every company." Richard Peters, also from Pennsylvania, spoke of it as "that erratic meteor which arose with so much splendor and I fear will set with no small disgrace." John Francis Mercer of Virginia, at the same period, wondered if it was not "a prostitution of the name of Government to apply it to such a vagabond, strolling, contemptible Crew as Congress...."[7]

The second common complaint is that other members are conceited, petty, and verbose: in a word, they talk too much. "The Congress do worse than ever," Charles Carroll of Maryland grumbled in April 1778: "We murder time, and chat it away in idle impertinent talk." In September of the same year John Mathews of South Carolina cried out: "Oh! my worthy friend, never was a Child more sick of a school, than I am, of this same business, I am sent here upon.... I have found the thirst for Chattering so extremely prevalent, that it absolutely disgusts me." Or as another disgruntled delegate put the matter in a striking phrase a couple of years later, Congress was "eternally penelopyzing." This comment came from Philip Schuyler of New York. His classical allusion was to Penelope, waiting for her husband Ulysses to return and laboriously unpicking the shroud she had woven in order to fend off her unwelcome visitors.[8]

The third complaint, also frequent and increasingly so as the war wore on, was of delegates' laxity in attendance. Sometimes it was necessary to wait for two or three weeks before a quorum could be assembled. When weather or accommodation or both were bad, only a handful of members might be present. Early in 1778, according to the President of Congress, Henry Laurens, there were "barely 9 States on the floor represented by as many persons."[9]

This does not sound like a bold collective leadership. Yet appearance may be deceptive. Some delegates were faithful in attendance and, like Samuel Adams or Elbridge Gerry of Massachusetts, put in several years of service. Thomas Burke of North Carolina believed that "power of all kinds has an irresistible propensity to increase a desire for itself. It gives the passion of ambition a velocity which increases in proportion as it is gratified." In Congress Dr. Burke was a consistent opponent of every move which he saw as likely to consolidate congressional authority at the expense of the states. But as governor of his own state in 1781, at a time of military emergency, he acted with such executive boldness that he clashed with the state board of war. No single generalization can fit the attitude of Congress to leadership.[10] All at one moment or another approved of some kinds of leadership and disapproved of others. Some, at the risk of platitude, hewed more or less to the same line. Sam Adams, for example, rarely said or wrote anything out of keeping with his basic position as an old-fashioned moralist. The old colonial government of Massachusetts, he wrote in 1780, had implanted bad habits of "political idolatry":

Such a temper is widely different from that reverence which every virtuous Citizen will show to the upright Magistrate. . . . May Heaven inspire the present Rulers [a curiously old-fashioned word?] with Wisdom & sound Understanding. In all Probability they will stamp the Character of the People.[11]

Other delegates, however, are perplexingly equivocal. John Mathews, in July 1778, was alarmed at the delay in ratifying the Articles of Confederation. He was sure that "if we are to have no Confederation until the Legislatures of the Thirteen States agree to one, . . . we shall never have one, and if we have not one, we shall be literally a rope of sand, and I shall tremble for the consequences that will follow at the end of this War." By October he was convinced that America was on the brink of ruin as a result of congressional dawdling:

I intend when I am about to leave C[ongress] to speak my mind very freely to them. . . , and shall conclude with telling them, . . . they are not calculated to conduct the business intrusted to them, and if the States do not fall upon some other mode, by which the concerns of the American States, are to be managed, we must inevitably fall to pieces, and that I intend to tell the State so I belong to, as soon as I go home, and will too.

In between July and October, however, Mathews' prime anxiety seemed to concern the risk that Congress would attempt to encroach on the sovereignty of the states.[12]

It rarely seems clear in many of these comments whether the lack or the excess of "leadership" is being complained about. Sometimes the same man appears to be worried about both. What are we to make, for example, of this diary entry by Thomas Rodney of Delaware in March 1781? After some unflattering descriptions of sundry colleagues, including James Madison of Virginia, Rodney observes that

> the affairs of the United States in Congress are not Conducted by the ablest talants and men of the first abilities. . . . Neither are they Conducted by the most true, disinterested and amiable spirit of Patriotism. Yet Congress Considered Collectively possesses a firm and Independant Spirit, with a determined and unalterable resolution to support the liberties of America. And tho selfish Conceit and opinions which most of the members possess has in some measure the effect of the most disinterested Patriotism, because it occasions them to disagree in every thing but those measures which is notoriously for the good of all, Yet this disjointed manner of proceeding throws government into that disorder'd tract of adopting one expedient after another perpetually by which means the States have lost their Credit, and Congress that Confidence which the People ought to have in their wisdom.

Rodney's clumsy prose makes one sigh for the lucidity of a Madison. But he is not stupid—he almost puts his finger on some subtle questions. The drift of his argument is, however, contradictory, through what I have called inherent confusion. Thus, Rodney believes the delegates are collectively second-rate, yet collectively courageous. Being conceited and particularistic, they damage the common cause in the name of the common cause. Yet, Rodney continues, such a variety of interests "as there must be among a people forming thirteen Independant States extended over a vast Tract of Country, and only connected by political ties, requires much time and experience to reduce them to Systematical order. . . ." So all apparently will be well—if the nation survives.[13]

If the contemporary record is puzzlingly equivocal, can historians put us straight? Yes, to a commendable degree. The researches of H. James Henderson present a convincing analysis of successive regional alignments in Congress. He identifies an eastern bloc, dominated by New England, which held the initiative from 1774 to 1779; then a middle-states bloc, dominant from about 1780 to 1783; and a final southern-states bloc, which made the running from about 1784. This approach throws a new light on politics in the Continental Congress and reminds us that there were important shifts of policy as well as personnel over the decade. Again, thanks to Samuel F. Bemis, Richard B. Morris, and others, we can now make good sense of how Congress and its emissaries conducted diplomacy. And E. James Ferguson has given us an admirable account of American public finance in the era of the Continental Congress.[14]

The whole picture, nevertheless, in my view remains indistinct. The history of Congress turns into other histories—of the states, of debts and currency, of political theory, of coalition warfare, of the governmental theory and practice that preceded 1774 and followed after Congress began to disintegrate in the mid-1780's. The concept of intellectual leadership, as I have already remarked, tends to hive off much of the early and the late cogitation of outstandingly reflective members of Congress, preempting their Founding Father role and leaving them to yawn round committee tables in obscurity. The concept of military leadership, as I have also said, tends to put the spotlight on General Washington and his associates— including those like Schuyler and John Sullivan who also served in Congress. It assigns a secondary and humdrum if not ignominious role to the delegates, rendering them vulnerable to the charges of having both badgered and neglected the army. We may feel it is not surprising that in the summer of 1779 John Dickinson of Pennsylvania and William Henry Drayton of South Carolina suddenly introduced a motion that "Congress immediately adjourn to the place where the Army shall be, and that the members shall respectively join the Militia, and act with them in such important operations as shall be judged most expedient for advancing the welfare of these States." At least they would then, so to speak, be where the action definably was.[15]

What I have been suggesting so far is that Congress could not contrive to disentangle problems of sovereignty, authority, leadership, and executive energy as problems in logic, because of the complexity and ambiguity of the terms they had to use and the value judgments that underlay them. I have also suggested that although excellent and dispassionate work has been done by historians on various facets, they have not in the nature of their inquiries produced a general synthesis of the history of the Continental Congress. There are two helpful surveys of Congress, by Edmund C. Burnett and Lynn Montross, but these are chronological rather than analytical in approach. Merrill Jensen's important book *The Articles of Confederation* (1940) is not a history of the Continental Congress, though it is an indispensable preliminary to such a volume.[16]

Oversimplifying somewhat, we can recognize two different broad interpretations of the era. They contradict one another but offer attractively plausible scenarios in themselves. According to the "nationalist" scenario, as exemplified in the writings of Claude H. Van Tyne, Congress was dilatory, inept, and cowardly. It shifted its location (shiftily) no less than seven times between December 1776, when it "fled" from Philadelphia to Baltimore, and the end of 1783, when it reopened temporarily at Annapolis. It grew steadily feebler and more factious as the war progressed, through its own incompetence and through having allowed the states to seize the initiative. The Articles of Confederation, not completed until

1777 and not finally ratified until 1781, were in any case inadequate; hence
the fortunate victory of common sense in replacing them by the 1787
Constitution. In this sort of exposition George Washington is the prime
hero, but Adams, Jefferson, Madison, and Hamilton can all be given high
marks. Since Congress is by definition a weak body, it hardly matters that
some of the ablest Founding Fathers seem to vanish into intellectual limbo
for a period after 1776. To the query of how Congress contrived to win
the war, the answer would more or less be that the war was won in spite
of Congress, by the army (with French help), by America's diplomats, and
through British blunders.[17]

The contrary position, most formidably represented by Merrill Jensen,
focuses upon the principled antipathy of "radical" Americans to centralized
power. He detects a quite fundamental conflict, originating well before the
war and continuing well past it, between "radicals" and "conservatives."
The former were the party of independence, democracy, and states' rights.
The latter were the party of conciliation, property, and centralized government. Jensen's thesis does not entail defending the executive efficiency of
the wartime Congress. Indeed he devotes little space to the delegates' military and diplomatic preoccupations, other than to examine how these bore
upon the ploys of congressional interest groups. I have no idea how he
would respond to the question of how Congress managed to win the war.
Within his own framework he would be entitled to dismiss it as meaningless or misconceived. I suppose, though, he might respond that many factors contributed to the outcome and that the states played a prominent part,
as they were expected to do by plenty of delegates in addition to men like
Thomas Burke and Sam Adams. The war was after all won by the United
States under the Confederation, as Patrick Henry insisted. By that test,
the Confederation was adequate for its purposes. The Jensen approach has
received reinforcement in recent years from historians sympathetic to radicalism. They are in general more concerned with decentralization than
with centralization and with resistance to rather than acceptance of authority. Neoradicalism would, I think, tend to regard "leadership" as an
elitist concept and would perhaps be more interested in "followership"—
that is, the role of the underdog in American history.[18]

What these two extremes share is a relative indifference to the ordinary
functioning of the Continental Congress. The one would dismiss it as a
story of malfunctioning. The other would concentrate on the tussle between
"radicals" and "conservatives," or possibly on the vitality of the states or
the nation at large.

Does this then mean that Adams and Jefferson were correct when they decided the history of the sessions behind "closed doors" could never be written? Have the ambiguities and the basic intellectual rivalries persisted down to the present day?

I have used up most of my time in raising obstacles. If a valuable new synthesis is to be written, I am not the person. All I can offer is some remarks toward a synthesis, beginning with points which would probably now be accepted by historians of whatever persuasion.

Thus, I believe much in the Jensen thesis is incontrovertible. The First Continental Congress of 1774 was a protesting body, not a formal legislature. The Congress that met in 1775 and in effect continued until 1789, less unified at the outset, derived its force from a dual challenge—a challenge to Britain and a challenge to the delegates who wished to stop short of independence. The activists in this Congress, such as the Adamses of Massachusetts, had convinced themselves that "the Administration," meaning the British government, was corrupt and tyrannical. They had abundant testimony, mainly from British sources, about corruption and a fair amount about tyranny, including the menace of standing armies. "Administration," with or without the prefatory article, became a dirty word for American revolutionists.[19] Remote governments manipulated by patronage were in their well-buttressed view innately dangerous, greedy, and corrupting as well as corrupt. In this broad proposition they were, I think, perfectly correct. Its relevance for our purpose is that the revolutionists who carried the day implanted in the American provisional government the belief that Congress itself would become dangerous and corrupt unless its scope and perhaps its duration were strictly and explicitly limited.

Moreover, in bringing on independence John Adams and his companions deliberately passed the initiative to the states. This vital move is outlined in a terse note from Adams to James Warren on May 15, 1776:

> This Day the Congress has passed the most important Resolution that ever was taken in America.
>
> It is as nearly as I can repeat it from Memory, in these Words. . . .
>
> *Resolved*—that it be recommended to the several Assemblies and Conventions to institute such Forms of Government as to them shall appear necessary, to promote the Happiness of the People.

The step was to some extent a tactical device to confront a hesitating Congress with a fait accompli—or rather with 13 faits accomplis. But it was entirely consonant with patriot thinking in America. The establishment of state governments was the first essential, and almost the whole essential. "Confederation among ourselves, or alliances with foreign nations," Adams told his wife Abigail on May 17, "are not necessary to a perfect separation from Britain." The "resolution for instituting governments" had brought that about, "to all intents and purposes." Confederation would, he assumed, be "necessary for our internal concord, and alliances may be so for our external defence." On June 23 Adams wrote exultantly to John Winthrop explaining how "the legislatures of the colonies" would exert themselves, displaying "a vigor hitherto unknown." He added:

> A committee is appointed to prepare a confederation of the colonies, ascertaining the terms and ends of the compact, and the limits of the Continental Constitution; and another committee is appointed to draw up a declaration that these colonies are free and independent States.[20]

The grand climax, for Adams, was the Declaration of Independence. To him and to Jefferson it was as much a culmination as a beginning. Separation from Britain was their proudest achievement in Congress. They took great pride in other activities, but as for what they went on to do in America itself during the lifetime of the Continental Congress, their contributions to Massachusetts and Virginia, respectively, seem to have been closest to their hearts. In the summer of 1776, though he anticipated a bloody war, Adams was almost blithe, as though he felt his own major part had already been played. When Congress had declared the colonies "free and independent States" and had sent ambassadors abroad, Adams wrote to an acquaintance on June 9, "I shall think that I have answered the end of my creation, and sing my *nunc dimittis,* return to my farm, family, ride circuits, plead law, or judge causes, just which you please."[21] If he was a leader, he was almost religiously determined not to posture on the national stage or to hold any office longer than was needful. His history of Congress, one suspects, would have been mainly a history of the years 1774–76.

Some of the other delegates were more candidly captivated by the leadership opportunities provided by the new nation. But the energy currents flowed into Congress from the states, not the other way round. Jack Greene's study of the lower houses of assembly in the southern colonies, *The Quest for Power,* shows that they "provided excellent training for the leaders" in Virginia, the Carolinas, and Georgia. These men, he says, were conspicuous in their own states and in Congress. Jackson Turner Main's book *The Sovereign States, 1775–1783* stresses the importance and the relatively long terms in office of the new state governors (except in Georgia); on average they served for nearly four years. There was a constant coming and going between Congress and the states. Delegates became members of legislatures, or governors, and vice versa.[22] After the Declaration of Independence, the most urgent domestic issue for Congress was to establish a basis of state representation. J. R. Pole comments that Congress could have solved the problem by agreeing with Patrick Henry that they were all Americans but adds that he was of course only speaking in a symbolic sense. In practice, provincial loyalties came first, as a matter of principle and because of the imbalance between large and small states. For whatever reasons, the outcome—one vote per state in Congress—diminished the claim of continentally minded Americans that Congress was the supreme representative body.[23] No doubt it also diminished the effectiveness of Congress. Since a delegate's personal vote counted for nothing, his temptation to stay away or arrive late was correspondingly increased. He was in any case, as Merrill Jensen reminds us, elected, paid for, instructed, and subject to recall by his state.[24] Men who felt that tension between equality and the desire to excel which is characteristic of democratic societies could satisfy both impulses by rising to the top in their own states, and perhaps also serving in Congress, without guilt and without arousing antagonism. With the adoption of the Articles, the theory of rotation in office also took effect in Congress. The rapid circulation of delegates hindered the development of institutional loyalty to that body. Congressional morale suffered in consequence. It was perhaps even more impaired by the discomforts and expense that delegates had to endure. But a reading of their often exasperated and woebegone letters indicates that a majority of members of Congress could not envisage a solution—at least, not one that would entail enlarging the powers of Congress. The adoption of the Articles was as far as they wished to go, up to 1781. After that, the urgency of reform seemed to depart.

Delegates were alarmed by the notion of interior conspiracies or "juntos," which smacked too much of British parliamentary corruption. H. James Henderson contends that these did exist. This was also the view of the French. La Luzerne, the French minister in Philadelphia, wrote to the French foreign minister Vergennes in May 1781 to explain how he had drawn John Sullivan into his confidence by means of a financial subsidy:

I have always found him disposed to be very confiding, and it is to him that I always attribute the rupture of the league formed by the Eastern States; a league which, by false ideas of popularity, of liberty, and by an excessive jealousy of the Army and of the General-in-Chief, has for so long a time delayed the most urgent measures, and which on numerous occasions has shown itself equally jealous of our advantages and of our influence.[25]

But such a communication makes La Luzerne sound more sinister than the eastern bloc. Successive blocs no doubt had their function in the embryonic national political system. During the lifespan of the Continental

Congress, however, it seems reasonable to suggest that one of their effects was to heighten mistrust between states, and therefore—in the context of the time—to lend credence to the fear that a "consolidated" government would entail the overlordship of some other state or region. This apprehension was eloquently put in a speech made in Congress in November 1778 by John Witherspoon of New Jersey:

One of the greatest dangers I have always considered the colonies as exposed to . . . , is treachery among themselves, augmented by bribery and corruption from our enemies. But what force would be added to the arguments of seducers, if they could say with truth, that it was of no consequence whether we succeeded against Great Britain or not; for we must, in the end, be subjected, the greatest part of us, to the power of one or more of the strongest or largest of the American states? [26]

Loyalty to Congress was thus qualified and reduced by all sorts of considerations. What of the nucleus of delegates who persisted in faithful attendance? They might conceivably have placed Congress first in their scheme of allegiances. The answer seems to be that they did not. Men who were seriously alienated tended like Philip Schuyler to leave and not come back. The faithful few grumbled but came back for more punishment. John Mathews of South Carolina, for example, after telling his friend Thomas Bee that he was sick to death of Congress halfway through his first session in 1778, kept serving until 1782. The regular attenders were so busy with committee work that they had no time to brood upon large schemes for the transformation of government. Andrew Adams of Connecticut, a newcomer in 1778, was awed and dazed by the press of business. Congress met, he said, at 10 a.m. and sat until 3, 4, or 5 p.m. Boards and committees convened either beforehand, as early as 6 a.m., or in the late afternoon when Congress adjourned. "I beleave there are but very few Members but what are employed in some of these Ways, so that those who do their duty have not much Leasure to spare." When Congress was in full blast it seems to have had something of the hectic bustle of a wartime munitions factory, in which daily output was the overriding element. Andrew Adams, at any rate, was suitably impressed (and remained a delegate until 1782). "I have as you observed," he wrote to a friend, "taken a Seat in Congress, and mixd among the great States-Men of America among whose shining Talents you may well imagine my feable Genious is lost in Obscurity. . . ." It is clear from the rest of his letter that he was not writing tongue-in-cheek. It is also clear that he regarded the other delegates as representatives of a far from unitary nation. He pictured to his friend "a house composed of very able and sensable Gentlemen: but belonging to different states, whose Laws, Manners, Genious and Inhabitants and indeed almost every thing else very different. . . ." A letter from Gouverneur Morris of New York, written on the same day, is less starry eyed but conveys the same picture of intense activity He was not enjoying himself, but he was worried because the only other delegate from New York, William Duer, threatened to leave—"so that, if I quit, the state will be unrepresented." The big states were particularly anxious to make their presence felt.[27]

All this is, I believe, a true picture of Congress. But it is not the whole truth. I am not thinking of the unedifying aspects, such as the bribery of John Sullivan by La Luzerne, or the muddles over army administration, or the prolonged squabble over the activities of Silas Deane, the American commissioner in Paris. These, after all, might have occurred under any form of government, consolidated or not. The subsequent history of Congress under the 1787 Constitution is not an entirely efficient or unblemished one. Nor is it possible to speculate very usefully on whether Congress might have supplied better leadership, given the atmosphere of America at the time. We can note in passing that historians who emphasize radicalism are apt to impute worthy motives to the so-called radicals and unworthy ones to the so-called conservatives. They do not seem anxious to tackle the question of whether ideological correctness might not have been harmful on occasion to American survival.

What I wish to comment on is the problem of semantic confusion. My point is not that if only Americans had clarified their language all would have been straightforward. That notion of salvation through semantics, which was in vogue some years ago, now seems naïve in the extreme. On the contrary: my argument is that the semantic confusion of the Congress era reveals a fundamental dilemma which has little to do with opposing teams of nationalists and republicans or conservatives and radicals. The dilemma, of course, was whether the United States was one country or 13—and, accordingly, what was the role of Congress. Much of the routine business of Congress could be carried on without having to face this issue. But it kept surfacing. Sometimes it could be dismissed as a mere legalistic conundrum. The British peace commissioners of 1778, for instance, did not get much satisfaction from their sly observation to Congress that "we . . . think ourselves entitled to a full Communication of the Powers by which you conceive yourselves Authorized to make Treaties with Foreign Powers." The commissioners remarked that although the Articles of Confederation (not yet ratified) conferred upon Congress the right to establish treaties and alliances, "we do not find promulgated any Act or Resolution of the Assembly's of particular States conferring this Power on you."

Even this dig, though, elicited a rather high-flown response—"Resolved that it is the indispensible Duty of Congress to claim and maintain the Dignities and Privileges aforesaid in their fullest Latitude and Comprehension."[28] In reaction to a foreign power, especially an enemy, Congress found itself compelled to assert its symbolic leadership of the whole United States. In other instances it seemed to fall flat on its face. Congress, for example, had little success in trying to discipline delegates who had broken the rules. In 1778 Thomas Burke was reprimanded for having withdrawn from a debate in order to break a quorum and refusing to return to the chamber. Charged with a breach of order, he declared that he would not submit to a "tyranny of a majority of this Congress, which would keep him here at unreasonable hours." He announced defiantly that he would hold himself accountable to North Carolina alone for his behavior in Congress. He was using "the freedom which according to my idea belongs to a Republican, and a representative of a Sovereign people." Congress considered expelling Burke, or committing him to jail. But he had gone off back to North Carolina, where he secured a hearty vote of support from the state legislature and was returned again to Congress.[29]

Nevertheless, in apparently trivial instances, we can detect signs of a felt need to stand up for the symbolic dignity of the United States, in the collective shape of Congress. One could hardly find a more devout states' righter than Samuel Adams. But he was outraged in the autumn of 1778 to hear from James Warren of the protocol surrounding the arrival in Boston of the French admiral d'Estaing. "Things," he declared, "which detachd and by themselves are justly considerd as Trifles light as Air, when they are . . . made Parts of a great Machine, become important. . . ." Adams' complaint was that in the toast list at a public entertainment, the "Monarch and Kingdom of France" preceded the "Congress." Moreover, separate 13-gun salutes had been fired in honor of France, the French army and navy, and General Washington and the army, but not to Congress. Adams was indignant also that the American army had been treated with greater courtesy than its civil masters and went into a diatribe about the dangers of suffering "the Civil to stoop to the Military Power."[30] Yet he was responding to these fancied slights on behalf of Congress. And in weightier situations, Congress was to continue to symbolize this national entity. As the war drew to an end and Congress began to seem on the verge of collapse, its symbolic leadership began to appear more and more necessary. It is true that the case for a stronger national government was being urged by some men of conservative temperament who had perhaps never quite emotionally accepted the rupture with Britain. Such buried Loyalism was,

however, rare. The consolidators now had a variety of reasons for wishing
to see America adequately represented via a central government. At the
state level as well as in Congress, certain of the arguments for minimal
government looked much less attractive than they had done. At the
national level, men who had been involved in issues transcending a single
state or region were naturally in favor of a government of more "adequate"
powers. So were younger men like Madison, who had come to Congress
after the great negations of 1774–76.[31] In those early days, leadership expressed itself as defiance, repudiation, risk. "Perhaps," as one delegate had
wryly observed in August 1776, "our Congress will be exalted on a high
gallows."[32] The spirit of '76 continued to inspire and to haunt Congress
through the war years. But other conceptions of leadership—some more
constructive, some more calculating—gradually came in beside them. I
think we can interpret some of the semantic confusions of Congress prose
in this light. Rival conceptions jostled.

It would be wrong to suggest that the confusions were or could be cleared
up at a stroke, in 1787 or any other year. The Continental Congress supplied an ancestry for American politics in more ways than one. Contradic-
tion, much of it healthy, remained a feature of the executive and legislative
scene. Andrew Jackson, the strong president who did not believe in a
strong presidency, is in direct line of descent from those earlier, bothered
men who wanted to be decisive without being dictatorial. So is Abraham
Lincoln. The essential ambiguity of leadership in a democracy is nicely
caught in that strange epithet "penelopyzing." The difference between
Philip Schuyler, who coined it, and some of the more radical delegates like
Thomas Burke is that Schuyler wanted Congress to stop penelopyzing and
provide the smack of firm government, whereas Burke resisted such a
remedy. In the long run neither quite got his way. That seems fitting, for
if we take the metaphor seriously, Burke was wise in his caution. Penelope,
that is, surrounded by grasping, dishonest people, was correct to refuse to
commit herself before Ulysses could arrive to rescue her. The problem for
both Burke and Schuyler—still our problem—was to decide who in the
American context could possibly be cast as Ulysses.

Notes

[1] Adams to Benjamin Rush, April 4, 1790, letterbook copy in Adams Papers, Massachusetts Historical Society; and *The Adams-Jefferson Letters,* ed. Lester J. Cappon,
2 vols. (Chapel Hill: Published for the Institute of Early American History and Culture

at Williamsburg, Va., by the University of North Carolina Press, 1959), 2:451, 452, 455. Punctuation modified for the sake of clarity.

[2] Gordon S. Wood, *The Creation of the American Republic, 1776–1787* (Chapel Hill: Published for the Institute of Early American History and Culture at Williamsburg, Va., by the University of North Carolina Press, 1969).

[3] *Letters of Members of the Continental Congress,* ed. Edmund C. Burnett, 8 vols. (Washington: Carnegie Institution of Washington, 1921–36; reprint ed., Gloucester, Mass.: Peter Smith, 1963).

[4] Merrill Jensen, *The New Nation; a History of the United States During the Confederation, 1781–1789* (New York: Knopf, 1950), pp. 362–63; Lynn Montross, *The Reluctant Rebels: The Story of the Continental Congress, 1774–1789* (New York: Harper, 1950), pp. 371–72.

[5] *Sources and Documents Illustrating the American Revolution, 1764–1788,* ed. Samuel Eliot Morison, 2d ed. (New York: Oxford University Press, 1965), pp. 315–16.

[6] Hamilton, *Vindication of Congress,* quoted in Montross, *Reluctant Rebel,* p. 361.

[7] Burnett, *Letters,* 1:528; Montross, *Reluctant Rebel,* pp. 354, 372.

[8] Edmund C. Burnett, *The Continental Congress* (New York: Macmillan, 1941), pp. 317–18; complaints by Mathews in Burnett, *Letters,* 3:420–21; Schuyler to George Washington, June 18, 1780, in Burnett, *Letters,* 5:224.

[9] Burnett, *Continental Congress,* p. 319.

[10] Material on Burke in Merrill Jensen, *The Articles of Confederation,* 3d ed. (Madison: University of Wisconsin Press, 1970), p. 174; and see Jensen, "The Articles of Confederation," in Library of Congress Symposia on the American Revolution, 2d, 1973, *Fundamental Testaments of the American Revolution* (Washington: Library of Congress, 1973), p. 72.

[11] Samuel Adams to Elbridge Gerry, November 27, 1780, in *The Writings of Samuel Adams,* ed. Harry A. Cushing, 4 vols. (New York & London: Putnam's, 1908), 4:228–30.

[12] Burnett, *Letters,* 3:322, 453.

[13] Rodney, "Caractors of Some of the Members of Congress," in Burnett, *Letters,* 6:19–22.

[14] H. James Henderson, "The Structure of Politics in the Continental Congress," *Essays on the American Revolution,* ed. Stephen G. Kurtz and James H. Hutson (Chapel Hill: Published for the Institute of Early American History and Culture by the University of North Carolina Press, 1973), pp. 157–96; Samuel Flagg Bemis, *The Diplomacy of the American Revolution* (Bloomington: Indiana University Press, 1957); Richard B. Morris, *The Peacemakers; the Great Powers and American Independence* (New York: Harper & Row, 1965); E. James Ferguson, *The Power of the Purse; a History of American Public Finance, 1776–1790* (Chapel Hill: Published for the Institute of Early American History and Culture at Williamsburg, Va., by the University of North Carolina Press, 1961).

[15] Burnett, *Continental Congress,* p. 392.

[16] The subtitle of Merrill Jensen's book is: *An Interpretation of the Social-Constitutional History of the American Revolution, 1774–1781.* Most of it is devoted to a discussion of the issues that determined the framing and then delayed the ratification of the Articles.

[17] See, for example, comments in Claude H. Van Tyne, *The War of Independence* (Boston: Houghton Mifflin, 1929), pp. 267–68.

[18] For a well-documented introduction to a neoradical interpretation, see Jesse Lemisch, "The American Revolution Seen From the Bottom Up," in *Towards a New Past: Dissenting Essays in American History,* ed. Barton J. Bernstein (New York: Vintage, 1969), pp. 3–45.

[19] General Nathanael Greene unwittingly enraged Congress by using the word to describe it in July 1780; Burnett, *Continental Congress,* pp. 462–63.

[20] Burnett, *Letters,* 1:445, 453, 502.

[21] Adams to William Cushing, in Burnett, *Letters,* 1:478.

[22] Jack P. Greene, *The Quest for Power; the Lower Houses of Assembly in the Southern Royal Colonies, 1689–1776* (Chapel Hill: Published for the Institute of Early American History and Culture at Williamsburg, Va., by the University of North Carolina Press, 1963), p. 361; Jackson Turner Main, *The Sovereign States, 1775–1783* (New York: New Viewpoints, 1973), pp. 190–91.

[23] Jensen, *Articles of Confederation,* pp. 140–45; J. R. Pole, *Political Representation in England and the Origins of the American Republic,* California Paperback Edition (Berkeley, Los Angeles, and London: University of California Press, 1971), pp. 345–53.

[24] Jensen, *Articles,* p. 141.

[25] Henderson, "The Structure of Politics in the Continental Congress," p. 169; Burnett, *Letters,* 4:307, footnote 2; Charles P. Whittemore, *A General of the Revolution, John Sullivan of New Hampshire* (New York: Columbia University Press, 1961), p. 177. A not altogether convincing answer to the "junto" accusation, probably written by Oliver Ellsworth of Connecticut (Burnett, *Letters,* 4:408–11), serves to remind us of the structural looseness of Congress:

"If you had only told us that Congress were a slow body, and let their business run behind hand no body would have questioned you; for we all know that such a body as Congress is can't move otherwise but slow. There are too many men, too many states represented, of different interests, customs and habits to get along with dispatch. And sometimes they will seem to be forever about a thing before they can get it into such a shape as suits them all; and it may be a small matter too. But this is no new thing under the sun; nor is there any help for it.

"If you had also . . . told us that Congress sometimes grow warm and have high debates, . . . this we could have believed to[o]; for the same happens in all free assemblies. . . .

"But that Congress should be ass riden with a junto is a matter that wants proof. . . . A wonderful work of great wickedness has been carrying on in Congress for five years and yet no mortal ever heard of it. . . . Another wonder in the matter is, that this wonderful combination has held its own so long. The members of Congress have been continually changing from the beginning, so that scarcely one of the first set are left behind. . . ."

This was written in 1779. By that year it was true that only a handful of delegates had continued to serve from 1774: Eliphalet Dyer and Roger Sherman from Connecticut; William Paca from Maryland; Samuel Adams from Massachusetts; James Duane and John Jay from New York; and Richard Henry Lee from Virginia. Montross, *Reluctant Rebels,* pp. 426–31.

[26] Burnett, *Letters,* 3:509.

[27] Burnett, *Letters,* 3:376–78.

[28] Burnett, *Letters,* 3:338.

[29] Burnett, *Continental Congress,* 306–9.

[30] Burnett, *Letters,* 3:457–58. The ambiguous response of Adams to the British commissioners is also interesting. An open reply to the Earl of Carlisle and others, first printed in the *Massachusetts Spy,* July 16, 1778, is attributed to Adams (*Writings of Samuel Adams,* ed. Cushing, 4:32–37). He speaks of the efficacy of American government as something apparently to be justified at state level. "Let me assure you, gentlemen, that the power of the respective Legislatures in each particular State is most fully established, and on the most solid foundations. It is established on the perfect freedom of legislation and a vigorous administration of internal government." However, he adds a much more comprehensively patriotic paragraph: "I subjoin the following creed of every good American:—I believe that in every kingdom, state, or empire there must be, from the necessity of the thing, one supreme legislative power, with authority to bind in every part. . . ." Adams addresses the British peace envoys as "An American." It is hard to believe that the good American's creed refers merely to the "supreme legislative power" in his own "particular State."

[31] This is a point stressed by Stanley Elkins and Eric McKitrick in their pamphlet *The Founding Fathers: Young Men of the Revolution* (Washington: Service Center for Teachers of History, 1962), pp. 23–26. The logic of the careers of Madison, Alexander Hamilton, and others "was in large measure tied to a chronology which did not apply in the same way to all the men in public life during the two decades of the 1770's and 1780's. A significant proportion of relative newcomers, with prospects initially modest, happened to have their careers opened up at a particular time and in such a way that their very public personalities came to be staked upon the national quality of the experience which had formed them. In a number of outstanding cases energy, initiative, talent, and ambition had combined with a conception of affairs which had grown immense in scope and promise by the close of the Revolution. There is every reason to think that a contraction of this scope, in the years that immediately followed, operated as a powerful challenge."

[32] Abraham Clark of New Jersey; Burnett, *Letters,* 1:528, footnote 2.

MARCUS CUNLIFFE has been professor of American studies at the University of Sussex since 1965. He read history at Oriel College, Oxford, with a four-year interlude as intelligence and reconnaissance officer in a tank battalion, and was a Commonwealth Fund Fellow in American History at Yale from 1947 to 1949. He began teaching American history and literature at the University of Manchester in 1949 and became professor of American history and institutions at Manchester in 1960.

His various stays in the United States have included a fellowship at the Center for Advanced Study in the Behavioral Sciences, Palo Alto, Calif. (1957–58), and visiting professorships at Harvard (1959–60), the City University of New York (1970), and the University of Michigan (1973).

Among his books are *The Literature of the United States* (1954), *George Washington: Man and Monument* (1958), *The Nation Takes Shape, 1789–1837* (1959), *Soldiers and Civilians: The Martial Spirit in America, 1775–1865* (1968, 1973), *American Presidents and the Presidency* (1969), and *The Age of Expansion, 1848–1917* (1974). He has edited *"The Life of Washington," by Mason L. Weems* (1962), *The Times History of Our Times* (1971), and, with Robin Winks, *Pastmasters: Some Essays on American Historians* (1968, 1975). Professor Cunliffe has contributed essays to several other books, and his reviews and articles have appeared in a variety of journals on both sides of the Atlantic. He is a member of the Massachusetts Historical Society, the Royal Historical Society, the British Bicentennial Liaison Commission, and a sprinkling of other organizations and committees.

Professor Cunliffe says that he does not possess a doctorate, earned or bestowed, and is not sure whether to boast of or to apologize for this nondistinction.

In 1969 appeared a historical study entitled The Creation of the American Republic. *On a heroic scale, of great subtlety of thought, and awesome in its scholarship, the book won numerous awards and was pronounced by a leading authority on the period "one of the half dozen most important books ever written about the American Revolution."*

The Creation of the American Republic *examines the political mind in America from 1763 to 1789. It concludes that, although the Federal Constitution was designed to check the popular excesses and experiments of the Revolutionary movement proper, it confirmed the boldest and most characteristically American experiment, whereby "the rulers had become the ruled and the ruled the rulers." "No more revolutionary change in the history of politics could have been made."*

The author of this remarkable book is Gordon S. Wood, professor of history at Brown University. In a similarly penetrating essay, written for this symposium, Professor Wood both compresses his earlier findings and extends them toward 1800. His argument is that the coming together of "ideas and power, intellectualism and politics," happened only once—in the Revolutionary era—and could never be repeated. For by bestowing ultimate political power on the whole body of the people the leaders of the Revolution ensured "their own demise."

There is a note of requiem in this that may not be acceptable to everyone. The expiration of the sedition law—the enactment of which, Mr. Wood believes, had been a last convulsive effort to retain power in the hands of an elite, where it had always been—did not end American contributions to political thought. Public opinion, to be sure, has often been tyrannous, and is always so in the hands of artful and unscrupulous men. But it has also been shaped into noble purposes by leaders thrown up from obscure origins by the democratic process. Abraham Lincoln is the classic instance.

Mr. Wood's closely reasoned paper deserves the most attentive reading not only for what it tells us about Americans then, but for what it suggests about the state of the Nation 200 years later.

The Democratization of Mind
in the American Revolution

GORDON S. WOOD

THE INTELLECTUAL CALIBER of the leaders of the American Revolution has never been in question. Praises of their qualities of mind have been sung so often that we are hard put to find new ways of describing them. In the last quarter of the 18th century, one historian has written, America "boasted a galaxy of leaders who were quite literally incomparable." "These leading representatives of the American Enlightenment," another historian has said, "were a cluster of extraordinary men such as is rarely encountered in modern history."[1] No one, it seems, can look back without being overawed by the brilliance of their thought, the creativity of their politics, the sheer magnitude of their achievement. They are indeed more marvellous than even those they emulated—the great legislators of classical antiquity—precisely because they are more real. They are not mythical characters but authentic historical figures about whom there exists a remarkable amount of historical evidence. For our knowledge of the Founding Fathers, unlike that of many of the classical heroes, we do not have to rely on hazy legends or poetic tales. We have not only everything the Revolutionary leaders ever published but also an incredible amount of their private correspondence and their most intimate thoughts, now being made available with a degree of editorial completeness and expertness rarely achieved in the long history of the West's recovery of its documentary past.

Despite the extent and meticulousness of this historical recovery, however, the Founding Fathers still seem larger than life and, from our present perspective especially, seem to possess intellectual capacities well beyond our own. The awe that we feel when we look back at them is thus mingled with an acute sense of loss. Somehow for a brief moment ideas and power, intellectualism and politics, came together—indeed were one with each other—in a way never again duplicated in American history. There is no doubt that the Founding Fathers were men of ideas and thought, in fact were the leading intellectuals of their day. But they were as well the political leaders of their day, politicians who competed for power, lost and won elections, served in their colonial and state legislatures or in the Congress, became governors, judges, and even presidents. Yet of course they were neither "intellectuals" nor "politicians," for the modern meaning of these terms suggests the very separation between them that the Revolutionaries avoided. They were intellectuals without being alienated and political leaders without being obsessed with votes. They lived mutually in the world of ideas and the world of politics, shared equally in both in a happy combination that fills us with envy and wonder. We know that something happened then in American history that can never happen again.

But there is no point now, 200 years later, in continuing to wallow in nostalgia and to aggravate our deep feelings of loss and present deficiency. What we need is not more praise of the Founding Fathers but more understanding of them and their circumstances. We need to find out why the Revolutionary generation was able to combine ideas and politics so effectively and why subsequent generations in America could not do so. With the proper historical perspective on the last quarter of the 18th century and with a keener sense of the distinctiveness of that period will come a greater appreciation of not only what we have lost by the passing of that Revolutionary generation but more important, what we have gained. For in the end what made subsequent duplication of the remarkable intellectual leadership of the Revolutionaries impossible in America was the growth of what we have come to value most—our egalitarian culture and our democratic society. One of the prices we had to pay for democracy was a decline in the intellectual quality of American political life and an eventual separation between ideas and power. As the common man rose to power in the decades following the Revolution, the inevitable consequence was the displacement from power of the uncommon man, the man of ideas. Yet the Revolutionary leaders were not merely victims of new circumstances; they were in fact the progenitors of these new circumstances: they helped create the changes that led eventually to their own undoing, to the breakup of the kind of political and intellectual coherence they represented. Without intending to, they eagerly destroyed the sources of their own sustenance and greatness.

There is no denying the power and significance of the intellectual products of the Revolutionary era. Samuel Eliot Morison and Harold Laski both believed that no period of modern history, with the possible exception of the Civil War decades of 17th-century England, was so rich in political ideas and contributed so much in such a short period of time to Western political theory.[2] In the Americans' efforts to explain the difference of their experience in the New World and ultimately to justify their Revolution and their new governments they were pressed to speak and write both originally and extensively about politics, using a wide variety of 18th-century instruments: newspapers, pamphlets, state papers, poetry, plays, satire and, of course, letters. Indeed, their phenomenal reliance on personal correspondence for the communication of their thoughts made the Revolutionary years the greatest letter-writing era in American history. (Without Jefferson's letters what would we know of his mind?) It is a remarkable body of political literature that the Revolutionaries created, and what is most remarkable about it is that this political theory was generally written by the very men responsible for putting it into effect.

Despite the intellectual creativity and productivity of the Revolutionary leaders, it is obvious that they were not professional writers. They bore no resemblance to the Grub Street scribblers hired by government officials to turn out political propaganda. Nor were they only men of letters, "intellectuals" like the 18th-century French philosophes or the Tory satirists of Augustan England, writers fully engaged in political criticism and using their pens to gain money and position. To be sure, there were American writers like John Trumbull and Philip Freneau who sought to make careers as littérateurs, but they were exceptions. Most of the intellectual leaders of the Revolution were amateurs at writing—clergymen, merchants, planters, and lawyers deeply involved in their separate occupations. Writing in fact was simply a byproduct of their careers and one of their many accomplishments or duties as gentlemen. Because they were gentlemen, they never wrote for money and rarely deigned to put their names on what they wrote for publication. They thought of their writing, even the belletristic sort, as a means to an end, either to make a polemical political point or to demonstrate their learning and gentlemanly status.

Yet men like James Otis, Richard Bland, Thomas Jefferson, and John Adams were not only amateur writers; in an important sense they were amateur politicians as well. For all the time and energy these Revolutionary leaders devoted to politics, most of them cannot accurately be described as professional politicians, at least not in any modern meaning of the term. Their relationship to public life and their conception of public service were different from those of today: their political careers did not create but rather followed from their previously established social positions; their political leadership, like their intellectual leadership, was a consequence, not a cause, of their social leadership. And thus they often saw their public service—sometimes wrongly, of course, but sincerely—as unhappy burdens, wretched responsibilities thrust upon them by the fact of their high social rank. Few of Jefferson's letters are as revealing and filled with emotion as his 1782 protest to Monroe over the social pressures making him engage in public service despite the miseries of office and his longing for private repose.[3] We smile today when we hear such protestations from politicians, but precisely because the 18th-century leaders were not professional politicians such disavowals of public office and such periodic withdrawals from politics as they habitually made possessed a meaning that is difficult for us today to recapture.

What ultimately enabled the Revolutionary leaders to be amateur politicians and amateur writers and to be both simultaneously was their status as gentlemen—the dominant social distinction of the 18th century that has since lost almost all of its earlier significance. They took their gentlemanly status seriously and accepted the privileges and responsibilities of the rank without guilt and without false humility. Compared to the English gentry of the 18th century, some of the colonial leaders may have been uncertain about their distinctive status, but none doubted the social importance of this distinctiveness, which was expressed in various ways—speech, dress, demeanor, learning, tastes, and one's acquaintances and friends. Eighteenth-century leaders took it for granted that society was a hierarchy of finely graded ranks and degrees divided vertically into interests and lines of personal influence, rather than as today into horizontal cleavages of class and occupation. In such a society men generally were acutely aware of their exact relation to those immediately above and below them but only vaguely conscious, except at the very top, of their connections with those at their own level. It was believed that the topmost rank, that of a gentleman—the only horizontal social division that had any significance to the 18th century —ought to have special sorts of men, the "better sort," men of property no doubt, but more—men of "good character." Members of the elite debated endlessly over what constituted the proper character for a gentleman— John Adams and Thomas Jefferson were still going at it in their correspondence at the end of their lives—but they never questioned the leadership of the society by an aristocracy of some sort. Because gentlemen saw themselves as part of an organic social community linked through strong personal connections to those below them, for all their feelings of superiority and elevation they had no sense of isolation from the society, no sense of standing in an adversary relationship to the populace. They were individuals undoubtedly, sometimes assuming a classic pose of heroic and noble preeminence, but they were not individualists, men worried about their social identities. They were civic minded by necessity: they thought they ought to lead the society both politically and intellectually—indeed, they could not help but lead the society—by the sheer force of their position and character. Ordinary men would respect and follow them precisely because the members of the elite possessed what ordinary men by definition could not have.

Because the Revolutionary leaders were gentry with special privileges and responsibilities, tied to the people through lines of personal and social authority, the character of their intellectual activity—what they wrote and spoke—was decisively affected. They believed that their speeches and writings did not have to influence directly and simultaneously all of the people but only the rational and enlightened part, who then in turn would bring the rest of the populace with them through the force of deferential respect. The politically minded public in 18th-century America may have been large compared to contemporary England, but most of the political literature of the period showed little evidence of a broad reading public. The Revolutionary leaders for the most part wrote as if they were dealing with reasonable and cultivated readers like themselves. Of course, by publishing their writings they realized they were exposing their ideas to the vulgar, which is why they usually resorted to pseudonyms, but yet they made very few concessions to this wider public. They still thought of the real audience for their intellectual productions as roughly commensurate with their social world. "When I mention the public," wrote John Randolph in a 1774 political pamphlet, "I mean to include only the rational part of it. The ignorant vulgar are as unfit to judge of the modes, as they are unable to manage the reins of government."[4] Such bluntness in public was rare and became even rarer as the Revolution approached. Although few of the Revolutionaries shared Randolph's contempt for the mass of the populace—indeed, most had little reason as yet to fear or malign the people—they vaguely held to a largely unspoken assumption that if only the educated and enlightened, if only gentlemen, could be convinced, then the rest would follow naturally.

Actually the reading public in the mid-18th century may have been more
limited than we have generally assumed. Certainly the prevalence of
literacy is no measure of it. The price of both newspapers and pamphlets
was itself restricting. Although a pamphlet cost no more than a shilling
or two, even that put it beyond the reach of most. Indeed, the practice of
reading some pamphlets before groups of Sons of Liberty or town meetings
indicates not the general breadth but the usual limits of their circulation.
Even members of the elite relied extensively on passing pamphlets from
hand to hand as if they were letters.[5]

Yet there is no doubt that the intellectual climate was changing in the
half century before the Revolution. In the 1720's there were fewer than a
half dozen newspapers in the colonies, with a limited number of sub-
scribers; by 1764 there were 23 newspapers, each with double or triple the
earlier circulation. Between 1741 and 1776 men had experimented with
at least 10 magazines, and although none of them lasted longer than a few
years, the effort was promising. Since most of the publications emphasized
governmental matters, there was bound to be some raising of political
consciousness, and printers were becoming more important public figures.
The number of political pamphlets multiplied at an ever-increasing rate,
and in some urban areas in the years before the Revolution such writings
were being used with particular effectiveness in election campaigning.[6]
All these developments were bringing Americans to the edge of a vast
transformation in the nature and size of their reading public and their
politically conscious society.

Regardless of the actual extent of the American reading public, what is
crucial is the Revolutionary leaders' consciousness of the elitist nature of
that public. We know they conceived of their readership as restricted and
aristocratic, as being made up of men essentially like themselves, simply by
the style and content of what they wrote. They saw themselves and their
readers as mutual participants in an intellectual fraternity, "the republic of
letters," a view that gave them a confidence in the homogeneity and the
intelligence of their audience which in turn decisively influenced the particular qualities of their literary productions.[7]

First of all, a large amount of the Revolutionary literature was extraordinarily learned, filled with Latin quotations, classical allusions, and historical
citations—multitudes of references to every conceivable figure in the heritage of Western culture from Cicero, Sallust, and Plutarch, to Montesquieu,
Pufendorf, and Rousseau. They delighted in citing authorities and in displaying their scholarship, sometimes crowding or even smothering the
texts of their pamphlets with quantities of footnotes.[8] Often the newspaper

essays and pamphlets were mere extensions of the kind of speeches that political leaders might present in legislative halls, devices by which gentlemen, in the absence of published reports of legislative debates, might tell other gentlemen what they said or would like to have said within the legislative chamber. Thus Stephen Hopkins' *The Rights of Colonies Examined* was first read before the assembly of Rhode Island, which then voted that it should appear in pamphlet form.[9] Or even more indicative of the limited elitist conception of the audience was the extraordinary reliance on personal correspondence for the circulation of ideas. It is often difficult to distinguish between the private correspondence and the public writings of the Revolutionaries, so much alike are they. Sometimes the published writings even took the form of letters or, like John Adams' pamphlet *Thoughts on Government,* grew out of what were originally letters to colleagues and friends.[10]

It is not just the prevalence of scholarship and the personal form of the literature that reveal the limited and elitist nature of the audience. Even the character of the invective and polemics suggests a restricted reading public in the minds of the authors. Much of the polemics was highly personal—a succession of individual exchanges between gentlemen who were known to one another, quickly becoming unintelligible to an outsider and usually ending in bitter personal vituperation. Since such abuse was designed to destroy the gentlemanly reputation of one's enemies, no accusation was too coarse or too vulgar to be made—from drunkenness and gambling to impotence and adultery.[11] The vitriolic burlesques, like those satiric closet dramas of Mercy Otis Warren, derived much of their force from the intimate knowledge the author presumed the audience or readers had of the persons being ridiculed or satirized. Without such familiarity on the part of the audience, much of the fun of the pieces—the disguised characterizations, the obscure references, the private jokes, the numerous innuendos—is lost.[12]

Indeed, it is the prevalence of satire in the Revolutionary literature that as much as anything suggests the elite nature of the audience. For satire as a literary device depends greatly on a comprehensible and homogeneous audience with commonly understood standards of rightness and reasonableness. Since the satirist can only expose to instantaneous contempt that which is readily condemned by the opinion of his readers, he must necessarily be on intimate terms with them and count on their sharing his tastes and viewpoint. If this intimacy should break down, if the satirist's audiences should become heterogeneous and the once-shared values become confused and doubtful—if the satirist has to explain what his ridicule means—then the satire is rendered ineffectual.[13] But most Revolutionary writers, at the outset at least, presumed the existence of these universal principles of right behavior and expected a uniformity of response, supposing that their audience either was or would like to be part of that restricted circle of men of good taste and judgment.

Nearly all the literature of the Revolutionary leaders thus reflected—in its form, its erudition, its polemics, its reliance on satire—a very different intellectual world from our own, a world dominated by gentlemen who were both amateur writers and amateur politicians, essentially engaged, despite their occasional condescension toward a larger public, in either amusing men like themselves or in educating men to be or think like themselves. More than any of these characteristics, however, what decisively separates the literature of the Revolutionary generation from that of our own was its highly rhetorical character. It was in fact the Revolutionaries' obsession with rhetoric and with its requirement of effectively relating to the audience in order to make a point that in the end helped contribute to the transformation of the American mind.

Rhetoric today no longer means what it meant to the 18th century. To us rhetoric suggests at best elocution, or at worst some sort of disingenuous pleading, hyperbolic bombast lacking the sincerity and authenticity of self-expression which we have come to value so highly. But to the Revolutionary generation rhetoric—briefly defined as the art of persuasion—lay at the heart of an 18th-century liberal education and was regarded as a necessary mark of a gentleman and an indispensable skill for a statesman, especially for a statesman in a republic. Language, whether spoken or written, was to be deliberately and adroitly used for effect, and since that effect depended on the intellectual leader's conception of his audience, any perceived change in that audience could alter drastically the style and content of what was said or written.[14]

Part of the remarkable effect created by Thomas Paine's *Common Sense*, for example, resulted from its obvious deepening of the layers of audience to whom it was directed. To be sure, it was a vigorously written pamphlet, filled with colorful, vivid language and possessing a fierce, passionate tone that no other American writer could match. And it said things about monarchical government that had not been said before; it broke through the presuppositions of politics and offered new ways of conceiving of government. But some of the awe and consternation the pamphlet aroused came from its deliberate elimination of the usual elitist apparatus of persuasion and its acknowledged appeal to a wider reading public. Paine's arguments are sometimes tortured, and the logic is often deficient. There are few of the traditional gentlemanly references to learned authorities and few of the subtleties of literary allusions and techniques known to the Augustans. Paine scorned "words of sound" that only "amuse the ear" and relied on a simple and direct idiom; he used concrete, even coarse and vulgar, imagery drawn from the commonplace world that could be understood even by the unlearned, and he counted on his audience being familiar with only one literary source, the Bible—all of which worked to heighten the pamphlet's potency and to broaden its readership, pointing the way toward a new kind of public literature.[15]

As the Revolutionary cause became more fervent and as the dimensions of the public that needed persuading expanded in men's minds, other kinds of changes appeared. Take, for example, the inflated emotions displayed in the annual public commemorations of the Boston Massacre that began in 1771 and continued on until 1784, when they were replaced by the equally grandiloquent orations celebrating the Fourth of July. Here is Joseph Warren speaking in 1775:

> Approach we then the melancholy walk of death. Hither let me call the gay companion; here let him drop a farewell tear upon that body which so late he saw vigorous and warm with social mirth—hither let me lead the tender mother to weep over her beloved son—come widowed mourner, here satiate thy grief; behold thy murdered husband gasping on the ground, and to complete the pompous show of wretchedness, bring in each hand thy infant children to bewail their father's fate—take heed, ye orphan babes, lest, whilst your streaming eyes are fixed upon the ghastly corpse, *your feet slide on the stones bespattered with your father's brains.*[16]

This sort of lurid exaggeration, this kind of sensational melodrama, strikes us today as incredible and indeed ludicrous. Yet we must remember that such oratorical utterances were rhetorical in a way that we can no longer appreciate, designed by the speaker not as an expression of his personal emotions but as a calculated attempt to arouse the emotions of his listeners. Rhetoric was the art of relating what was said and how it was said to the needs and requirements of the audience. Since the speaker or writer aimed above all to make a point and sway his public, rhetoric was necessarily less concerned with the discovery of the truth than with the means of communicating a message. Not that the truth was to be falsified or perverted; everyone assumed that rhetoric was to be the servant of truth and that the good orator or writer, the good statesman, had to be a good man—which is one reason why 18th-century gentlemen so carefully guarded their personal reputations. But it is clear, simply from the examples of Paine and Warren, that the demands of persuading and adapting to an audience, especially when that audience was perceived as diffuse and vulgar, could break through the usual stylized rules of rhetoric and lead both to a new kind of directness and commonness of expression and to the kind of verbal excesses and emotional extravagance that increasingly came to mark much of American public utterance in the decades following the Revolution.

Such an art, such a use of rhetoric, resembling our modern notion of propaganda, seems to us dangerous because we are not as confident as the Revolutionaries were that the audience will be, in Jefferson's words, "an assembly of reasonable men." What ultimately justified the 18th century's use of rhetoric and kept it from becoming propaganda as we know it was the intellectual leaders' civic sense of being part of the network of society with responsibility for the welfare of that society and of having an intimate and trusted relationship with their rational audiences. Society was the only measure of man; all his writing, all his utterances, all his intellectual and artistic activity had preeminently a social and hence rhetorical function. Even Jefferson's intense efforts to create a classical style for America's public buildings flowed from his sense of the social significance of architecture. Of all the arts architecture was the most rhetorical because, as Jefferson put it, it was "an art which shows so much." Hence all sorts of other considerations—including function and cost—could be sacrificed for the sake of the elevating effects a replica of a Roman temple would have on its viewers.[17]

In such a rhetorical world the intellectual leader had no business standing apart from the society in critical or scholarly isolation. Thus someone like Benjamin Franklin never thought the role of closet scientist, no matter how distinguished, compared in significance with that of public servant. Franklin in fact saw his whole life and career in rhetorical terms: all of his artful posing, his role-playing, his many masks, his refusal to reveal his inner self—all these characteristics followed from Franklin's obsessive civic-consciousness and his intense awareness that he was a persona in a drama whose actions and statements would profoundly affect his audience.[18] Today we are instinctively repelled by such calculation, such insincerity, such willingness to adapt and compromise for the sake of society; yet our distaste for such behavior is only one more measure of our distance from the Revolutionary era.

★   ★   ★

That 18th-century rhetorical world, that neoclassical world of civic-minded philosopher-statesmen, is now clearly gone. But it was going even then, even as it expressed itself most forcefully and brilliantly. While the Revolutionary gentry were still busy creating their learned arguments to persuade reasonable men of the need for resistance or of the requirements of government, there were social processes at work that would in time undermine both their political and intellectual authority. A new democratic society was developing, becoming both a cause and a consequence of the Revolution. As egalitarian as American society was before 1776, as broad as the suffrage was in the several 18th-century colonies, the republican society and culture that gradually emerged after the Declaration of Independence were decidedly different from what had existed earlier. The older hierarchical and homogeneous society of the 18th century—a patronage world of personal influence and vertical connections whose only meaningful horizontal cleavage was that between gentlemen and common people—this old society, weaker in America and never as finely calibrated as in England, now finally fell apart, beset by forces released and accelerated by the Revolution, to be replaced over the subsequent decades with new social relationships and new ideas and attitudes, including a radical blurring of the distinction between gentlemen and the rest of society. New men, often obscure ordinary men, were now touched by the expanding promises of opportunity and wealth in post-Revolutionary America and clamored for a share in the new governments and in the economy. The "people" were now told repeatedly that they rightfully had a place in politics, and lest they should forget, there were thousands of new rising popular tribunes, men who lacked the traditional attributes of gentlemanly leaders, to remind them, cajole them, even frighten them into political and social consciousness. Under such pressures, within a generation or so after Independence the old 18th-century world was transformed: the gentry, at least outside the South, gradually lost its monopoly of politics and intellectualism as the audience for politicians, writers, and orators ballooned out to hitherto unimaginable proportions.

Although few of these changes actually began with the Revolution, it was during the Revolution that they became evident. Before the Revolutionary movement only a few Americans, mostly royal officials and their connections, had worried about the expanding size of America's political society. But the imperial controversy had the effect of making all Americans more conscious of the power of the people out of doors. Political leaders, in their contests with royal authority, vied with each other in demonstrating their superior sympathy with the people—and in the process considerably widened and intensified their public audience.[19] Given the Whig tradition of celebrating the people against the Crown, it was a tendency that most American leaders found difficult to resist. In 1766 the Massa-

chusetts House of Representatives erected a public gallery for the witnessing of its debates—a momentous step in the democratization of the American mind. The Pennsylvania Assembly followed reluctantly in 1770, and
eventually the other legislatures too began to reach out to a wider public,
usually provoked by the desire of Whig leaders to build support among
the people for opposition to Great Britain.[20] Yet old habits died hard and
it was difficult to shed the conception of assembly proceedings being in the
nature of private business among gentlemen. Votes in the legislatures continued to remain unrecorded and reports of debates were rarely carried to
the outside world. When in 1776 the Revolutionaries met in their conventions to discuss the forms of their new state constitutions, they felt no
need either to report what they said or to extract vows of secrecy to prevent leaks of what they said to the people out of doors. As a result we
know very little of what went on during those momentous closed meetings
in the months surrounding the Declaration of Independence. Apparently
the leaders believed that nearly everyone who counted and ought to hear
what was said was within the legislative or convention halls.

A decade later, however, by 1787, the situation had become very different. In many of the states, particularly in Pennsylvania and Massachusetts,
legislative debates had begun to be reported by a growing number of newspapers (which now included dailies) and political leaders had developed a
keen, even fearful, awareness of a larger political society existing outside
of the legislative chambers. Politics no longer seemed an exclusively gentlemanly business, and consequently gentlemen in public discussions increasingly found themselves forced to concede to the popular and egalitarian
ideology of the Revolution, for any hint of aristocracy was now pounced
upon by emerging popular spokesmen eager to discredit the established
elite leaders. Under these changed circumstances the delegates to the
Philadelphia Convention in 1787 felt it necessary to take extraordinary
measures to keep their proceedings private: no copies of anything in the
journal were allowed, nothing said in the Convention was to be released
or communicated to the outside society, and sentries were even to be
posted to prevent intruders—all out of a sensitivity to a public out of doors
that had not existed 10 years earlier.

By the late 1780's gentlemen in the Convention had become convinced
not only that this public—"the too credulous and unthinking Mobility,"
one delegate called it—was now interested in what went on within doors
but that, if allowed access to the debates through publication by "im-
prudent printers," this hovering presence of the people would inhibit the
delegates' freedom of expression.[21] Events bore out the significance of this

deliberate decision to impose secrecy. The delegates to the Philadelphia Convention showed a remarkable degree of candor and boldness in discussing what were now sensitive issues, like aristocracy and the fear of popular power, that was notably missing from the debates in the various ratifying conventions held several months later. Since the ratifying conventions were open and their proceedings widely publicized in the press, the difference in the tone and character of the respective debates is revealing of just what a broader public could mean for the intellectual life of American politics. Madison later reportedly declared that "no Constitution would ever have been adopted by the convention if the debates had been public."[22] As it was, the defenders of the proposed Constitution knew very well that "when this plan goes forth, it will be attacked by the popular leaders. Aristocracy will be the watchword; the Shibboleth among its adversaries."[23] Hence the proponents of the Constitution found themselves in the subsequent public debates compelled to stress over and over the popular and "strictly republican" character of the new federal government. Men who only a few months earlier had voiced deep misgivings over popular rule now tried to outdo their opponents in expressing their enthusiasm for the people. "We, sir, idolize democracy," they said in answer to popular critics of the Constitution.[24]

Although aspects of this public exuberance by the Federalists over the democratic character of the Constitution appear disingenuous and hypocritical to us in light of their private fears of popular power, in the debates they were only doing what their liberal education in rhetoric had taught them: adapting their arguments to the nature and needs of their audience. Yet the demands of rhetoric were not supposed to lead to dishonesty and duplicity by the intellectual leader, particularly if his audience was the people. Such a gap between private and public feelings as was displayed in the debates over the Constitution only raised in a new form an issue that had been at the heart of American public discussions throughout the 18th century, and never more so than at the time of the Revolution.

During that entire century, and even earlier, enlightened men everywhere had been obsessed by what was often called "Machiavellian duplicity," the deliberate separation between men's hidden feelings or motives and their public face—an obsession that the rhetorical attitude only enhanced. It was taken for granted that men could and would assume roles and play falsely with their audience or public. The worst villain was the one who, like Iago, achieved his end through plots and dissembling; indeed, the enlightened 18th century was incapable of locating evil anywhere else but in this kind of deceiving man.

Assumptions like these lay behind the character of American political life in the 18th century and eventually became central to the decision to revolt in 1776. Time and time again, opposition spokesmen against royal authority in the colonies had emphasized the duplicity and flattery of courtiers who selfishly sought the favor of great men while they professed service to the public. Dissimulation, deception, design were thus accusations quickly made, and suspicion of men in power pervaded the political climate. The alternative to the courtier, opposition spokesmen said, was the true patriot, a man like themselves who did not need to dissemble and deceive because he relied solely on the people. As the conventional theory of mixed government pointed out, the people may have lacked energy and wisdom, but they made up for these deficiencies by their honesty and sincerity. Hence writers and critics, themselves gentlemen, delighted in posing as simple farmers or ploughjoggers in attacking the aristocratic pretensions and duplicity of other gentlemen who had acted condescendingly or who seemed to possess privileges and powers they had no right to have—all the while citing in support of their arguments 18th-century writers from Richardson to Rousseau who were increasingly celebrating the moral virtue of sincerity, or the strict correspondence of appearance and reality, action and intention.

At the beginning of the Revolution few American Whig gentlemen had any deep awareness that, in drawing these contrasts between the aristocratic guile and pretensions of the rank they belonged to or aspired to and the sincerity and honest hearts of the body of common people, they were unleashing a force they could not control. In 1776 many of them, including the likes of John Adams and Thomas Jefferson, watched with equanimity and indeed enthusiasm the displacement in political office of proud and insolent grandees by new men "not so well dressed, nor so politely educated, nor so highly born...." There was little to fear from such a "political metamorphosis," to use Jefferson's term, for these new men were "the People's men (and the People in general are right). They are plain and of consequence less disguised,...less intriguing, more sincere."[25]

Out of these kinds of changes in values, fed by the vast social transformation taking place on both sides of the Atlantic, developed a new sentimentalization of the common man and of natural and spontaneous speech. In this atmosphere the use of Greek and Latin as the exclusive property and ornament of gentlemen was disparaged and the written and spoken word itself became suspect, as men, taking off from Locke's mistrust of imagery, increasingly urged that what was needed in communication were things, not words.[26] And since words, not to mention the classical languages, were associated with cultivated learning and with aristocracy, it was the common man, the simple untutored farmer or even, in the eyes of some like Jefferson, the uncorrupted Indian with his natural gift of oratory, who became consecrated. It was not long before all gentlemen, those "lawyers, and men of learning and money men, that talk so finely, and gloss over matters so smoothly," were brought into question.[27]

By the final decade of the 18th century the implications of what was happening were becoming clear to some American gentry. Growing apprehensions over the abuses of popular power had contributed to the movement to create the new federal government, and such fears of democracy eventually became the fixation of the Federalist party in the 1790's. Most Federalist leaders, at least those who were old enough to be politically conscious at the time of the Revolution, had not anticipated becoming afraid of the people. Like other good Whigs, they had assumed that the people, once free of English influence, would honor and elevate the country's true patriots and natural aristocracy in ways that the English Crown had not. But when in the decades following the Revolution the people seemed to succumb to the deceit and flattery of mushrooming demagogues, who were the popular counterparts of courtiers, the Federalists became bewildered and bitter. All respectability, all learning, all character—the very idea of a gentleman as a political leader—seemed to be under assault.

The Federalist writers and speakers of the 1790's responded as 18th-century gentlemen would—with the traditional elitist weapons of satire and invective, saturating the political climate with vituperation and venom the likes of which has never been equaled in our national history. But such verbal abuse and ridicule—against democracy, demagoguery, vulgarity— were rhetorical devices designed for a different culture than America was creating. Such calumny and invective as the Federalists expressed were supposed to be calculated and deliberately exaggerated, not a genuine expression of the satirists' inner emotions, and were justifiable because they were the result of the righteous indignation that any gentleman would feel in similar circumstances.[28] Hence to be effective such rhetorical anger and abuse were dependent on an instantaneous uniformity of recognition by the audience of the universal principles of truth and reasonableness to which the satirist appealed. But the democratization of American society and culture that was occurring in these years was not only broadening and diversifying the public, weakening those common standards of rightness and good behavior that underlay the potency of satire; it was destroying the ability of the Federalist writers to maintain a rhetorical detachment from what was happening. The Federalists thus groped during the next decade or so to discover a rhetoric that could persuade their audience without at the same time alienating it.

The Federalists found it increasingly difficult to publicly speak the truth as they saw it and not get punished for it. Anonymity was now resorted to less because it was unseemly for a gentleman in the eyes of other gentlemen to expose his writings to the vulgar than because it was harmful for a gentleman's public career in the eyes of the vulgar (who could vote) to be caught writing, especially if that writing contained anything unpopular.[29] "In democracies," the Federalists concluded, "writers will be more afraid *of* the people, than afraid *for* them," and thus the right principles of political science, like those that had been discovered by the Revolutionary leaders, would become "too offensive for currency or influence" and America's intellectual contributions to politics would cease.[30] Some Federalists took a stubborn pride in their growing isolation from the public, regarding scorn by the people as a badge of honor and counting on posterity to vindicate their reputations.[31] Other Federalists, however, could not easily abandon their role as gentlemanly leaders and sought desperately to make their influence felt, some eventually concluding that they too must begin flattering the people, saying that if they could not achieve their ends "but by this sort of *cant,* we must have recourse to it." They came to realize, in Hamilton's words, that "the first thing in all great operations of such a government as ours is to secure the opinion of the people." But in competition with their Republican opponents the Federalists, said Fisher Ames, were like "flat tranquility against passion; dry leaves against the whirlwind; the weight of gunpowder against its kindled force."[32] They could not shed fast enough their traditional 18th-century rhetorical and elitist techniques. They continued to rely on a limited audience of reasonable gentlemen like themselves who alone could respond to their satirical blasts against democracy and vulgarity. And they preferred private correspondence among "particular gentlemen" to dealing with the unlettered multitude through the newly developing media of communication, especially the newspapers.[33]

In the 1790's both the Federalists and their opponents recognized the changing role popular media of communication were coming to play in American public life.[34] The sale of every sort of printed matter—books, pamphlets, handbills, periodicals, posters, broadsides—multiplied, and through new channels of distribution these publications found their way into hands that were not used to such literature. In New York City alone the number of booksellers increased from five in 1786 to 30 by 1800.[35] No vehicle of communication was more significant than newspapers; in time men of all persuasions came to believe that the press was almost single-handedly shaping the contours of American political life. The number of newspapers grew from fewer than 100 in 1790 to over 230 by 1800; by 1810 Americans were buying over 22 million copies of 376 newspapers annually, the largest aggregate circulation of newspapers of any country in the world.[36] With this increase in readership came a change in the newspaper's style and content. Although much of the press, especially that in Federalist control, retained its 18th-century character, other papers began responding to the wider democratic public. Prices were reduced, new eye-catching typography was used, cartoons appeared, political information replaced advertisements on the front pages, political speeches, debates, and rumors were printed, editorials were written, and classical pseudonyms were dropped as "a friend of the people" or "one of the people" became more attractive signatures. In most public writing there was a noticeable simplification and vulgarization: the number of footnotes, the classical and literary allusions, the general display of learning all became less common, as authors sought, in the way Paine had, to adapt to the new popular character of their readers.[37]

Not all gentlemen in the 1790's became Federalists of course, nor did all gentlemen become apprehensive over what was happening. Jefferson and the other gentlemen who came to constitute the Republican leadership retained a remarkable amount of the earlier Whig confidence in the people and in what Jefferson called the "honest heart" of the common man. Part of this faith in democracy on the part of Jefferson and his Republican colleagues in the South can be attributed to their very insulation from it, for most of the southern planters remained comparatively immune to the democratic electoral politics that were beginning to seriously disrupt northern society and to eat away the popular deference to "the better sort" that the southern gentry took for granted.[38] Moreover, because these democratic developments in the North—not only the new popular literature and the broadened public but the expanded suffrage, the new immigrants, the mobilization of new men into politics—all tended to support the Republican cause, they seemed unalarming to Republican gentlemen everywhere and only vindications of their trust in the people and fulfillments of the Revolution.

Nevertheless, the Republican intellectual leaders at first showed little more knowledge than the Federalists did in dealing with an expanded

American public. To be sure, Jefferson, in good Enlightenment manner, had always favored the full exchange of ideas and almost alone among the Founding Fathers had disliked the Philadelphia Convention delegates' "tying up the tongues of their members"—a decision, he said, which only reflected "their ignorance of the value of public discussion." And right at the outset of the 1790's Madison had urged as being favorable to liberty and republican government the development of "whatever facilitated a general intercourse of sentiments," such as roads, commerce, frequent elections, and "particularly *a circulation of newspapers through the entire body of the people.*"[39] But during the 1790's, when the popularization of American culture was proceeding rapidly, Jefferson continued to rely extensively on private correspondence for the dissemination of his views, and Madison continued to write learned pieces, like his "Helvidius" essays, for a restricted audience of educated gentlemen.

Others, however, hundreds of writers and speakers, common ordinary obscure men, men without breeding, without learning, without character— in short, persons who were not gentlemen—were now presuming "without scruple, to undertake the high task of enlightening the public mind." By 1800, wrote the Reverend Samuel Miller in his elaborate compendium of the Enlightenment entitled *A Brief Retrospect of the Eighteenth Century,* much of the intellectual leadership of America had very recently fallen into "the hands of persons destitute at once of the urbanity of gentlemen, the information of scholars, and the principles of virtue."[40] And these intellectual upstarts were for the most part supporting the Republican party, and in their literature were exceeding even the Federalists in scurrility and vituperation and reaching out to touch an audience as obscure and ordinary as themselves.

To the Federalists this upstart nature of both authors and audience was precisely the point of their frenzied response to the literature of the 1790's. It was one thing to endure calumny and abuse from one's own social kind. That had been a constant part of Anglo-American political life for a century or more. But it was quite another thing to suffer such invective from social inferiors, from nongentlemen, from "uneducated printers, shop boys, and raw schoolmasters," and to have such criticism and vituperation carried down to the lowest levels of the society.[41] Like freethinking and deistic religious views, such personal abuse was socially harmless as long as it was confined to the gentlemanly ranks. But when it spread to the lower orders, as it was doing in the 1790's at the hands of Republican publications, it tended to destroy the governing gentry's personal reputation for character and the deferential respect for the rulers by the common people on which the authority of the political order was based. It was these considerations—the belief that the channels of communication between governors and governed were rapidly becoming poisoned by mushroom intellectual leadership and the fear that the stability of the entire political order was at stake —that lay behind the Federalists' desperate resort to coercion, the sedition law of 1798—an action which more than anything else has tarnished their historical reputation. The Federalists' attempt to stop up the flow of malice and falsehood from the Republican presses by the use of state power may have been desperate, but it was not irrational, as the subsequent debate over the Sedition Act showed. For at issue in the debate was not simply freedom of the press but the very nature and structure of America's intellectual life.

The debate over the Sedition Act marked the crucial turning point in the democratization of the American mind. It fundamentally altered America's understanding not only of its intellectual leadership but of its conception of public truth. The debate, which spilled over into the early years of the 19th century, drew out and articulated the logic of America's intellectual experience since the Revolution, and in the process it undermined the foundations of the elitist 18th-century classical world on which the Founding Fathers stood.

In the discussions over the sedition law the Republican libertarian theorists rejected both the old common law restrictions on the liberty of the press and the new legal recognition of the distinction between truth and falsity of opinion which the Federalists had, they thought, generously incorporated into the Sedition Act. While the Federalists clung to the 18th century's conception that "truths" were constant and universal and capable of being discovered by enlightened and reasonable men, the Republicans argued that opinions about government and governors were many and diverse and their truth could not be determined simply by individual judges and juries, no matter how reasonable such men were. Hence they concluded that all political opinions—that is, words as distinct from overt acts—even those opinions that were "false, scandalous, and malicious," ought to be allowed, as Jefferson put it, to "stand undisturbed as monuments of the safety with which error of opinion may be tolerated where reason is left free to combat it." [42]

The Federalists were incredulous. "How . . . could the rights of the people require a liberty to utter falsehood?" they asked. "How could it be right to do wrong?" [43] It was not an easy question to answer, as we are recently finding out all over again. The Republicans felt they could not deny outright the possibility of truth and falsity in political beliefs, and thus they fell back on a tenuous distinction, developed by Jefferson in his first inaugural address, between principles and opinions. Principles, it seemed, were hard and fixed, while opinions were soft and fluctuating; therefore, said Jefferson, "every difference of opinion is not a difference of principle." The implication was, as Benjamin Rush suggested, that individual opinions did not count as much as they had in the past, and for that reason such individual opinions could be permitted the freest possible expression.[44]

What ultimately made such distinctions and arguments comprehensible was the Republicans' assumption that opinions about politics were no longer the monopoly of the educated and aristocratic few. Not only were true and false opinions equally to be tolerated but everyone and anyone in the society should be equally able to express them. Sincerity and honesty, the Republicans argued, were far more important in the articulation of ultimate political truth than learning and fancy words that had often been used to deceive and dissimulate. Truth was actually the creation of many voices and many minds, no one of which was more important than another, and each of which made its own separate and equally significant contribution. Solitary individual opinions may thus have counted for less, but in their numerous collectivity they now added up to something far more significant than had ever existed before. When mingled together they resulted in what Americans now obsessively labelled "public opinion"—a conception that soon came to dominate all of American intellectual life.[45]

Public opinion is so much a part of our politics that it is surprising that we have not incorporated it into the Constitution. We constantly use the term, seek to measure whatever it is and to influence it, and worry about who else is influencing it. Public opinion exists in any state, but in our democracy it has a special power. The Revolution in America transformed it and gave it its modern significance. By the early years of the 19th century Americans had come to realize that public opinion, "that invisible guardian of honour—that eagle eyed spy on human actions—that inexorable judge of men and manners—that arbiter, whom tears cannot appease, nor ingenuity soften—and from whose terrible decisions there is no appeal," had become "the vital principle" underlying American government, society, and culture.[46] It became the resolving force not only of political truth but of all truth—from disputes among religious denominations to controversies over artistic taste. Nothing was more important in explaining and clarifying the democratization of the American mind than this conception of

public opinion. In the end it became America's 19th-century popular substitute for the elitist intellectual leadership of the Revolutionary generation.

Although the will of the people, the vox populi, was an old idea in
Western culture, it took on an enhanced significance in the latter part of
the 18th century in response to the steady democratization of Western
society. During the Revolutionary era many American leaders, echoing
Hume and other enlightened thinkers, had become convinced that public
opinion ought to be "the real sovereign" in any free government like
theirs. Yet when Madison in 1791 referred to public opinion he was still
thinking of it as the intellectual product of limited circles of gentlemen-
rulers. Which is why he feared that the large extent of the United States
made the isolated individual insignificant in his own eyes and made easier
the counterfeiting of opinion by a few.[47] Other Americans, however, were
coming to see in the very breadth of the country and in the very insig-
nificance of the solitary individual the saving sources of a general opinion
that could be trusted.

Because American society was not an organic hierarchy with "an intellectual unity," public opinion in America, it was now argued, could not
be the consequence of the intellectual leadership of a few learned gentlemen. General opinion was simply "an aggregation of individual sentiment,"
the combined product of multitudes of minds thinking and reflecting independently, communicating their ideas in different ways, causing opinions
to collide and blend with one another, to refine and correct themselves,
leading toward "the ultimate triumph of Truth." Such a product, such a
public opinion, could be trusted because it had so many sources, so many
voices and minds, all interacting, that no individual or group could manipulate or dominate the whole.[48] Like the example of religious diversity in
America, a comparison many now drew upon to explain their new confidence in public opinion, the separate opinions allowed to circulate freely
would by their very differentness act, in Jefferson's word, as "a Censor"
over each other and the society—performing the role that the ancients and
Augustan Englishmen had expected heroic individuals and satiric poets to
perform.[49]

The Americans' belief that this aggregation of individual sentiments,
this residue of separate and diverse interacting opinions, would become the
repository of ultimate truth required in the end an act of faith, a faith
that was not much different from a belief in the beneficent workings of
providence. In fact, this conception of public opinion as the transcendent
consequence of many utterances, none of which deliberately created it, was
an aspect of a larger intellectual transformation that was taking place in

these years. It was related to a new appreciation of the nature of the social
and historical process being developed by Western intellectuals, particularly
by that brilliant group of Scottish social scientists writing at the end of the
18th century. Just as numerous economic competitors, buyers and sellers
in the market, were led by an invisible hand to promote an end which
was no part of their intent, so too could men now conceive of numerous
individual thinkers, makers and users of ideas, being led to create a result,
a public opinion, that none of them anticipated or consciously brought
about.

In such a world, a democratic world of progress, providence, and innumerable isolated but equal individuals, there could be little place for the
kind of extraordinary intellectual leadership the Revolutionary generation
had demonstrated. Because, as Americans now told themselves over and
over, "public opinion will be much nearer the truth, than the reasoning
and refinements of speculative or interested men," because "public opinion
has, in more instances than one, triumphed over critics and connoisseurs"
even in matters of artistic taste, because, as the Federalists warned, public
opinion was "of all things the most destructive of personal independence
& of that weight of character which a great man ought to possess," because
of all these leveling and democratizing forces, it was no longer possible
for individual gentlemen, in their speeches and writings, to make themselves felt in the way the Founding Fathers had.[50]

In the new egalitarian society of the early 19th century, where every
man's opinion seemed as good as another's, either "men of genius" (they
could no longer be simply educated gentlemen) became "a sort of outlaws,"
lacking "that *getting-along* faculty which is naturally enough the measure
of a man's mind in a young country, where every one has his fortune to
make"; or, in trying to emulate the civic-consciousness of the Founding
Fathers, such would-be intellectual leaders ended up being "fettered by
fear of popular offence or [having] wasted their energies and debased
their dignity in a mawkish and vulgar courting of popular favor."[51] It was
not a world many of the Founding Fathers would have liked, but they
would have at least understood it. For it was their creation, and it was
rooted in the vital force that none of them, Federalists included, ever could
deny—the people. In the end nothing illustrates better the transforming
democratic radicalism of the American Revolution than the way its intellectual leaders, that remarkable group of men, contributed to their own
demise.

Notes

[1] Henry Steele Commager, "Leadership in Eighteenth-Century America and Today," *Daedalus* 90 (1961): 652; Adrienne Koch, ed., *The American Enlightenment* (New York: George Braziller, 1965), p. 35.

[2] Samuel Eliot Morison, ed., "William Manning's *The Key of Libberty,*" *William and Mary Quarterly,* 3d ser. 13 (1956): 208.

[3] Jefferson to Monroe, 20 May 1782, in Adrienne Koch and William Peden, eds., *The Life and Selected Writings of Thomas Jefferson* (New York: Random House, Modern Library, 1944), p. 56.

[4] [John Randolph], *Considerations on the Present State of Virginia* (n.p., 1774), quoted in Merrill Jensen, "The Articles of Confederation," in Library of Congress Symposia on the American Revolution, 2d, 1973, *Fundamental Testaments of the American Revolution* (Washington: Library of Congress, 1973), p. 56.

[5] Homer L. Calkin, "Pamphlets and Public Opinion during the American Revolution," *Pennsylvania Magazine of History and Biography* 64 (1940): 30, 35.

[6] Frank Luther Mott, *American Journalism: A History: 1690–1960,* 3d ed. (New York, The Macmillan Co., 1962), pp. 3–64; F. L. Mott, *A History of American Magazines, 1741–1850* (New York: D. Appleton and Co., 1930), pp. 13–67; Arthur M. Schlesinger, *Prelude to Independence: The Newspaper War on Britain, 1764–1776* (New York: Vintage, 1965), pp. 51–66, 303–4; Philip Davidson, *Propaganda and the American Revolution, 1763–1783* (Chapel Hill: University of North Carolina Press, 1941).

[7] References to the republic of letters are common in the Revolutionaries' writings. See, for example, Brooke Hindle, *The Pursuit of Science in Revolutionary American, 1735–1789* (Chapel Hill: Published for the Institute of Early American History and Culture, Williamsburg, Va., by the University of North Carolina Press, 1956), p. 384.

[8] Bernard Bailyn, *The Ideological Origins of the American Revolution* (Cambridge: Harvard University Press, 1967), p. 23.

[9] Calkin, "Pamphlets and Public Opinion," *Pennsylvania Magazine of History and Biography* 64 (1940): 28, 35.

[10] John Adams, *Diary and Autobiography,* ed. L. H. Butterfield et al., 4 vols. (Cambridge: Harvard University Press, 1961), 3:331–32.

[11] Bailyn, *Ideological Origins,* pp. 4–5, 17.

[12] John J. Teunissen, "Blockheadism and the Propaganda Plays of the American Revolution," *Early American Literature* 7 (1972):148–62.

[13] Maynard Mack, "The Muse of Satire," in Richard C. Boys, ed., *Studies in the Literature of the Augustan Age; Essays Collected in Honor of Arthur Ellicott Case* (New York: Gordian Press, 1966).

[14] On 18th-century rhetoric see Wilbur Samuel Howell, *Eighteenth-Century British Logic and Rhetoric* (Princeton: Princeton University Press, 1971); Peter France, *Rhetoric and Truth in France: Descartes to Diderot* (Oxford: Clarendon Press, 1972);

Warren Guthrie, "The Development of Rhetorical Theory in America, 1635–1850," *Speech Monographs* 13 (1946): 14–22; 14 (1947): 38–54; 15 (1948): 61–71.

[15] Bernard Bailyn, "Common Sense," in Library of Congress Symposia on the American Revolution, *Fundamental Testaments*, pp. 7–22; Paine, *Common Sense* (1776), in *The Complete Writings of Thomas Paine*, ed. Philip S. Foner, 2 vols. (New York: The Citadel Press, 1969), 1:8; James T. Boulton, *The Language of Politics in the Age of Wilkes and Burke* (London: Routledge and Kegan Paul, 1963), chap. 7.

[16] Joseph Warren, "Oration Delivered at Boston, March 6, 1775," in H. Niles, ed., *Principles and Acts of the Revolution in America* . . . (Baltimore: Printed and published for the editor by W. O. Niles, 1822), p. 20.

[17] Eleanor Davidson Berman, *Thomas Jefferson Among the Arts: An Essay in Early American Esthetics* (New York: Philosophical Library, 1947), pp. 210, 130.

[18] Franklin to Cadwallader Colden, October 11, 1750, in *The Papers of Benjamin Franklin*, vol. 4, ed. Leonard W. Labaree et al. (New Haven: Yale University Press, 1961), p. 68; Robert F. Sayre, *The Examined Self: Benjamin Franklin, Henry Adams, Henry James* (Princeton: Princeton University Press, 1964), pp. 12–43.

[19] Gary B. Nash, "The Transformation of Urban Politics, 1700–1765," *Journal of American History* 60 (1973): 605–32.

[20] J. R. Pole, *Political Representation in England and the Origins of the American Republic* (London: St. Martin's Press, 1966), pp. 69–70, 277–78.

[21] Alexander Martin to Governor Caswell, July 27, 1787, in Max Farrand, ed., *The Records of the Federal Convention*, 4 vols. (New Haven: Yale University Press, 1911–37), 3:64.

[22] Jared Sparks: Journal, April 19, 1830, ibid., 3:479.

[23] John Dickinson, ibid., 2:278.

[24] John Marshall (Va.), in Jonathan Elliot, ed., *The Debates in the Several State Conventions on the Adoption of the Federal Constitution*, 2d ed., 5 vols. (Washington, 1836–45), 3:222; Gordon S. Wood, *The Creation of the American Republic, 1776–1787* (Chapel Hill: Published for the Institute of Early American History and Culture, Williamsburg, Va., by the University of North Carolina Press, 1969), pp. 524, 562–64.

[25] John Adams to Patrick Henry, June 3, 1776, in *The Works of John Adams . . .*, ed. Charles Francis Adams, 10 vols. (Boston: Little, Brown and Co., 1850–56), 9:387–88; Thomas Jefferson to Benjamin Franklin, August 13, 1777, in *The Papers of Thomas Jefferson*, ed. Julian P. Boyd et al. (Princeton: Princeton University Press, 1950–), 2:26; Roger Atkinson to Samuel Pleasants, November 23, 1776, quoted in James Kirby Martin, *Men in Rebellion: Higher Governmental Leaders and the Coming of the American Revolution* (New Brunswick, N.J.: Rutgers University Press, 1973), p. 190.

[26] Meyer Reinhold, "Opponents of Classical Learning in America During the Revolutionary Period," *Proceedings of the American Philosophical Society* 112 (1968): 221–34; Linda K. Kerber, *Federalists in Dissent: Imagery and Ideology in Jeffersonian America* (Ithaca: Cornell University Press, 1970), pp. 95–134.

[27] Amos Singletary (Mass.), in Elliot, ed., *Debates*, 2:102.

28 George L. Roth, "American Theory of Satire, 1790–1820," *American Literature* 29 (1958): 399–407; Roth, "Verse Satire on 'Faction,' 1790–1815," *William and Mary Quarterly*, 3d ser. 17 (1960): 473–85; Bruce I. Granger, *Political Satire in the American Revolution 1763–1783* (Ithaca: Cornell University Press, 1960), p. 2.

29 Robert E. Spiller et al., *The Literary History of the United States*, 3d ed. (New York: Macmillan Co., 1963), p. 175; Benjamin Spencer, *The Quest for Nationality: An American Literary Campaign* (Syracuse: Syracuse University Press, 1957), p. 65.

30 Fisher Ames, "American Literature," *Works of Fisher Ames*, ed. Seth Ames, 2 vols. (Boston: Little, Brown and Co., 1854), 2:439–40.

31 Richard Buel, Jr., *Securing the Revolution: Ideology in American Politics, 1789–1815* (Ithaca: Cornell University Press, 1972), p. 113; Gerald Stourzh, *Alexander Hamilton and the Idea of Republican Government* (Stanford: Stanford University Press, 1970), pp. 95–106.

32 John Rutledge, Jr., to Harrison Gray Otis, April 3, 1803, quoted in David Hackett Fischer, *The Revolution of American Conservatism: The Federalist Party in the Era of Jeffersonian Democracy* (New York: Harper and Row, 1969), p. 140; Alexander Hamilton to Theodore Sedgwick, February 2, 1799, in *The Works of Alexander Hamilton*, ed. Henry Cabot Lodge, 12 vols. (New York: G. P. Putnam's Sons, 1903), 10:340; [Fisher Ames], "Laocoon. No. 1," in his *Works*, 2:113.

33 Thomas Truxtun to John Adams, December 5, 1804, quoted in Fischer, *American Conservatism*, pp. 133–34.

34 Donald H. Stewart, *The Opposition Press of the Federalist Period* (Albany: State University of New York Press, 1969), pp. 634, 638, 640.

35 Sidney I. Pomerantz, *New York: An American City, 1783–1803* (Port Washington, N.Y.: Ira J. Friedman, 1965), p. 440.

36 Mott, *American Journalism*, p. 167; Merle Curti, *The Growth of American Thought*, 3d ed. (New York: Harper and Row, 1964), p. 209; Stewart, *Opposition Press*, pp. 15, 624.

37 Fischer, *American Conservatism*, pp. 129–49; Stewart, *Opposition Press*, p. 19; Jere R. Daniell, *Experiment in Republicanism: New Hampshire Politics and the American Revolution, 1741–1794* (Cambridge: Harvard University Press, 1970), pp. 235–36.

38 Buel, *Securing the Revolution*, pp. 75–90.

39 Jefferson to John Adams, August 30, 1787, in Farrand, ed., *Records of the Federal Convention*, 3:76; Madison, "Public Opinion," *National Gazette*, December 19, 1791, in *The Writings of James Madison*, ed. Gaillard Hunt, 9 vols. (New York: G. P. Putnam's Sons, 1900–10), 6:70.

40 Samuel Miller, *A Brief Retrospect of the Eighteenth Century . . . .* 2 vols. (New York: Printed by T. and J. Swords, 1803), 2:254–55.

41 Fisher Ames to Jeremiah Smith, December 14, 1802, quoted in Fischer, *American Conservatism*, p. 135.

42 [George Hay], *An Essay on the Liberty of the Press . . .* (Philadelphia: Printed at the Aurora office, 1799), p. 40; Jefferson, Inaugural Address, March 4, 1801, *Writings of Jefferson*, p. 322.

[43] Samuel Dana, Debates in Congress, January 1801, quoted in Buel, *Securing the Revolution*, p. 252.

[44] Jefferson, Inaugural Address, March 4, 1801, *Writings of Jefferson*, p. 322; Rush to Jefferson, March 12, 1801, *Letters of Benjamin Rush*, ed. Lyman H. Butterfield, 2 vols. (Princeton: Princeton University Press, 1951), 2:831.

[45] Tunis Wortman, *A Treatise Concerning Political Enquiry, and the Liberty of the Press* (New York: Printed by G. Forman for the author, 1800), pp. 118–23, 155–57.

[46] William Crafts, Jr., *An Oration on the Influence of Moral Causes on National Character, Delivered Before the Phi Beta Kappa Society, on Their Anniversary, 28 August, 1817* (Cambridge, Mass.: University Press, Hilliard and Metcalf, 1817), pp. 5–6; Wortman, *Treatise*, p. 180.

[47] Madison, "Public Opinion," *National Gazette*, December 19, 1791, *Writings of Madison*, 6:70.

[48] Wortman, *Treatise*, pp. 118–19, 122–23.

[49] Jefferson to John Adams, January 11, 1816, in Lester J. Cappon, ed., *The Adams-Jefferson Letters*, 2 vols. (Chapel Hill: Published for the Institute of Early American History and Culture, Williamsburg, Va., by the University of North Carolina Press, 1959), 2:458.

[50] Samuel Williams, *The Natural and Civil History of Vermont*, 2d ed., 2 vols. (Burlington, Vt.: Printed by Samuel Mills, 1809), 2:394; Joseph Hopkinson, *Annual Discourse, Delivered Before the Pennsylvania Academy of the Fine Arts* ... (Philadelphia: Bradford and Inskeep, 1810), p. 29; Theodore Sedgwick to Rufus King, 11 May 1800, quoted in Richard E. Welch, Jr., *Theodore Sedgwick, Federalist: A Political Portrait* (Middletown, Conn.: Wesleyan University Press, 1965), p. 211.

[51] [Richard Henry Dana, Sr.], "Review of the Sketch Book of Geoffrey Crayon, Gent.," *North American Review* 9 (1819):327; Theron Metcalf, *An Address to the Phi Beta Kappa Society of Brown University, Delivered 5th September, 1832* (Boston, 1833), p. 6.

GORDON S. WOOD, professor of history at Brown University since 1969, has also taught at the University of Michigan (1967–69) and at Harvard University (1966–67). From 1964 to 1966 he was a Fellow at the Institute of Early American History and Culture at Williamsburg, Va., and taught at the College of William and Mary. His publications include *The Creation of the American Republic, 1776–1787* (1969), which was nominated for the National Book Award for History and Biography in 1970 and received the Bancroft and John H. Dunning Prizes in 1970, *Representation in the American Revolution* (1969), and *The Rising Glory of America, 1760–1820* (1971). He is currently working on a study of American culture in the periods of the Revolution and the early republic.

Professor Wood received an A.B. degree from Tufts University in 1955 and M.A. and Ph.D. degrees from Harvard University in 1959 and 1964, respectively. From 1955 to 1958 he served in the U.S. Air Force in Japan. He is a member of the American Historical Association Committee for the Bicentennial Celebration of the American Revolution and has served on the editorial board of the *Journal of American History*.

It was the military history of the Revolution that most strongly attracted writers and readers when, early in the 19th century, young America paused long enough to write and read history. Generals published memoirs; biographers—sometimes the sons or grandsons of their subjects—lauded the triumphs of American commanders in the field; antiquaries traced campaigns in their states or regions from Bennington to Savannah. "Washingtonolatry" flourished. The Reverend Joel T. Headley's Washington and His Generals (1847) went through innumerable editions. Benson J. Lossing conducted a one-man industry producing popular books on Revolutionary heroes, battles, and sites. A reviewer said of Lossing's Pictorial Field-Book of the Revolution (1852) that it was "destined to find its way to every farmer's hearth and to all the school libraries in our country." Apparently it did.

A principal task of 20th-century military historians has been stripping away the accretions of myth and sentiment these books had laid down. One approach they have used is to study armies and their leaders in the context of the society they served and from which they sprang. Don Higginbotham, professor of history at the University of North Carolina, is one of the ablest exponents of this method. In his present closely packed but lucid essay, he sets forth the social and moral presuppositions of the American officer corps, points out the parallels and contrasts with those prevailing in European armies, and shows why, despite the felt threats of the affair at Newburgh in 1783 and the establishment of the Society of the Cincinnati, no military coup occurred, no military caste got a foothold in the United States.

"All action," Charles Francis Adams wrote in 1856, "must be measured by a standard formed by comparing the difficulties in which men are involved with the facilities provided to overcome them." Mr. Higginbotham finds no great concentration of military genius among the American military commanders collectively; in fact he finds relatively little below the level of Washington and Greene. But he does single out for the highest praise their resourcefulness and success, against fantastic odds, in keeping their armies in being. Their endurance, together with the aid supplied by France, was what won the war. On the basis of evidence rather than folklore, Professor Higginbotham's exposition thus restores some of the laurels too readily bestowed and then taken away in the last century and a half.

Military Leadership
in the American Revolution

DON HIGGINBOTHAM

HE WHO HAZARDS AN ABSOLUTE, ironclad definition of military leadership is likely to be in for trouble, and doubtless the same warning applies to other fields of leadership as well. Indeed, one may argue that the same qualities make up a successful leader regardless of his profession. No less a firsthand authority than General of the Army Omar N. Bradley has seen similar requirements for high military officers and captains of industry. Likewise, the distinguished British military historian General J. F. C. Fuller claimed that only a fine line separates the essential characteristics of the great soldier and the political statesman, an opinion seconded by the late David Potter, a careful student of the American Civil War.[1]

Clausewitz, the eminent German scholar-soldier, already sensed at the time of his writing in the early 19th century what had become obvious to subsequent commentators such as Bradley, Potter, and Fuller. To direct major campaigns, wrote Clausewitz, required great insight into the political objectives of the state. It was there that war and politics merged and the leader in the field became the statesman.

These sentiments were not of a piece with European military thought in the 18th century: By later standards, much of it was romantic and anti-professional. The Comte Guibert, Marshall Saxe, and William Lloyd argued that a general was born, not made. The higher portion of military knowledge was inbred; it was natural or intuitive. "Application rectifies ideas," declared Saxe, "but does not furnish a soul, for that is the work of nature."[2]

It was somewhat easy to adhere to romantic conceptions when the methods of warfare were anchored to the slimmest of theoretical under-pinnings. Officers, professional in name, were really amateurs. Britain had no Sandhurst; France, no St. Cyr. It is, of course, important to ask when a society reaches the point in its development where professionalism re-places amateurism in the most crucial fields of endeavor. In Western societies specialization has followed increases in population and techno-logical advancement, which have in turn brought a need for more exten-sive education and training. To be sure, that process was well under way in the Old World by the 18th century. But if what might be termed the tutorial or apprenticeship methods—those based on direct practical experi-ence—dominated education in law, medicine, and military affairs in the English colonies, it should be remembered that they had not disappeared altogether in Europe, notwithstanding the presence of such institutions as the Inns of Court, the universities with their medical curricula, and a cluster of artillery schools. Karl Demeter, after investigating the Prussian officer cadre, observed that despite the lip service given to formal education in science and mathematics as helpful to the understanding of linear for-mations or reducing fortresses under siege, service in the field was still considered to be infinitely more valuable.[3]

So too it was in the British army, where, according to Sir Henry Clinton, there was considerable rivalry between the so-called German and American schools, the former composed of officers who had fought with Frederick on the continent in the Seven Years' War, the latter consisting of the subordinates of Braddock, Wolfe, and Amherst in the phases of that con-flict occurring in the colonies.

Since the Age of Reason, under the spell of Newtonian physics and its broad intellectual implications, tended to see knowledge in wholes rather than in parts, one may more easily understand why military phenomena also remained largely undifferentiated. Logistics were only dimly under-stood, and the word itself had yet to enter the language. The difference between strategy and tactics was imprecisely recognized. If employed at all, the word *strategy* must have been uttered sparingly; so far as is known, it was foreign to Washington. *Stratagem* occasionally appears in the litera-ture of the period, but it was stated to mean a ruse, a manner of gaining a surprise. By the time of the American Revolution, the expressions *grand tactics* and *elementary tactics* were sometimes in evidence. The former, however, was not really equivalent to modern strategy—it seems to have been confined to the movements of troops beyond or outside the direct area of battle.

Consequently, lacking a body of strategic doctrine, officers could scarcely analyze a problem in systematic fashion, could hardly choose from a store of military principles certain options for practical application. Subordinate officers found little opportunity for initiative and independent judgment when everything revolved around the central figure, when strict obedience was expected by one who supposedly held mystical, knightly attributes. Thus the times were anything but conducive to the development of a staff-and-command system in which the primary objective is enunciated and individual commanders are given a measure of leeway in achieving it. Instead, the officers around the commander in chief were a loosely knit group, known as his "family," whose job it was to carry out the business of headquarters.

If the training and duties of the quasi-professionals, the engineers and artillerymen, were rather precise, it was nonetheless true that when they were lucky enough to advance to the senior ranks they likely found themselves assigned to administrative commands. At best, officers in all the military branches possessed a set of techniques—easily learned and available to all—which qualified them as narrow craftsmen of the battlefield, where the linear formation, the fire by volley, and the bayonet charge ruled the day.

Yet it would be erroneous to say there was no talk of innovation in warfare, of greater employment of skirmish groups and individual aimed fire in certain circumstances. The process of change was a slow, evolutionary one, however, and—with the possible exception of the French army—it had made relatively little headway by 1775. The limits to flexibility and rapid movement as late as 1806 may be illustrated in the person of Hans von Yorck, himself a military reformer and commander of the most mobile regiment in the Prussian army, who began the campaign of that year "encumbered with three trunks, two crates, two bedrolls, a bedstead with mattresses and bedding, and dozens of other items."[4] It has been suggested that if Marlborough had been restored to life at the end of the 18th century, he would have encountered "comparatively little with which he was not already familiar."[5]

In no small measure, innovation was retarded by the fear that social change would inevitably accompany it. And a cardinal tenet of the age was the belief that only the chosen few should dominate the vital sectors of the state. Aristocrats alone possessed what Frederick the Great called a true sense of honor. They, and none others, were inbred with a moral compunction which drove them—out of respect for themselves, their calling, and their sovereign—to endure hardship and confront danger and death without faltering. Commoners did not face the threat of family ostracism as did noblemen, who had a standard of honor to live up to. The bourgeoisie was too materialistic, too rational in the face of danger. Although Frederick allowed bourgeois officers a place in his army during the Seven Years' War, he afterward labored to eliminate from the officer corps this inferior substance. By shortly after 1800 the Prussian army's officer contingent of some 7,000 men included fewer than a thousand from outside the nobility, and these objectionables were largely confined to the artillery and other subsidiary branches of the service.

Frederick's Prussia was not unique, for almost everywhere the lesser nobility, hard-pressed to sustain themselves on their estates, sought preferment and its accompanying rewards in the military establishments. This situation contrasted sharply with that of the previous century, when in some countries army service had been a vehicle for men of low birth to achieve prominence and thus move upward on the social pyramid, even to the point of obtaining nobility for themselves and their descendants.

In 1764, the Marquis de Crenolles wrote that officers should originate in "the purest part of the nation." He explained that "if one of them had not been born with honour in his blood, the fear of losing caste, the shame which would result for his family, would act as a check on him and to some extent replace what he might lack in courage. Certainly it is only the nobility who are like that."[6] To the Chevalier d'Arc, a bastard grandson of Louis XIV and author of *La Noblesse Militaire* (1756), the army should be the sole possession of the superior caste in the state, which of course was the nobility.

In France a royal ordonnance of 1781 required most newcomers to the officer station to provide evidence of purely noble ancestry on their father's side for the last four generations, a requirement that was not completely original but actually more a tightening of earlier efforts to eliminate impurities. And if such restrictions were never completely enforced, promotion to the higher officer echelons did become almost rigidly the preserve of the courtiers.

In England the picture was not markedly different, although the nobility shared the officer enclave with the gentry and one also found a sprinkling of officers' sons and Huguenots. On the whole, however, the Hanoverian kings were no more willing to place talent above social origin than Frederick or Louis XVI. All three Georges took great interest and pride in the army, which could be led only by officers whose loyalty to the Crown was unquestioned since their troops might be needed to control the social order. As William Willcox notes, military station "was part of an older world that was still insulated and beyond the reach of the mercantile and industrial interests. Generals were more directly responsible to the King than most civilian officials, and had to be acceptable to him because they depended upon his favor for advancement."[7]

Duty and honor were allegedly the hallmarks of a British aristocrat who sought to make his contribution to the "public interest" by military service, an officer who not ashamedly might also expect fame and fortune since they were the natural preserve of the natural ruling class. If members of the British elite, in and out of the army, often failed to live up to the ideals associated with their order—as was true of Sir William Howe, who found solace in the easy life rather than fulfilling the promise of his youth—their code of behavior nevertheless exercised a powerful influence on men's minds. The sister of Lord Cornwallis, referring to her own son, said that "his honor is much dearer to me than his life."[8] Influenced by their families, by their education at Eton and Westminster, and by the church, the sons of the aristocracy grew to full manhood in the belief that they were by right of birth destined to rule and defend the nation. Or as Wellington said, he belonged to that race of gentlemen in the country which had endowed Britain with its glory and prosperity.

★　★　★

Now for the American Revolutionists, for what they thought about military leadership. Did the Revolutionary crisis expose basic differences between Englishmen and Americans in the military realm that had been unrecognized or inadequately perceived earlier? And were they as great as the political dichotomies over such matters as representation and constitutionalism that Bernard Bailyn has described for us?

Americans shared with their English cousins (but not with most continental Europeans) the concept of civil control of the military, though the patriots saw this age-old safeguard threatened by the presence of redcoats in the colonies on the eve of conflict and by the appointment of Gen. Thomas Gage as governor of the colony of Massachusetts in 1774. Too often, as David Hume had warned, the warrior had been burned by the flames of fame and had turned to the subversion of empires, the devastation of provinces, and the sacking of cities. In seeking a commander for the newly formed American army, the Continental Congress found no military genius on the horizon—no Hannibal, Wallenstein, Turenne, Marlborough, or Saxe—and doubtless they wanted none in view of their anti-

Caesar complex. In short, the Revolution was not to be the lengthened shadow of a single man.

For the most part, however, American military thinking generated no radical departure from conventional norms. The colonists generally shared in the assumptions widely held throughout most of the Western world that high station was the preserve and responsibility of those with more than ordinary capacity. Yet Americans believed that an office itself, be it a political or a military one, scarcely possessed qualities of its own. Rather, the right kind of men gave dignity and luster to their offices. Or, to put it a slightly different way, the character of the office-holder defined the office. (Later, by the Jacksonian period, Americans would view offices more impersonally, defining them by rules and regulations.)[9]

To be sure, America had no nobility, nor were there impenetrable barriers between segments of society, but in every colony there were men whose wealth, talent, education, experience, and family background, or some combination thereof, set them apart, men who constituted a kind of homegrown aristocracy. To a large degree, Congress and the states initially turned to such men for their general officers—to a Washington, a Schuyler, a Ward, and so on—and for their junior and field grade officers as well— to a Lewis Morris, a Henry Beekman Livingston, a Henry Lee, a John Laurens, a Joseph Habersham. Washington, himself courtly and retiring and abhoring familiarity between men of high and low station, was convinced that gentlemen alone made worthwhile officers, if only they could elicit respect as men of character and influence. So too it was that gentlemen of their position must be counted on to remain with the army at critical times, even to the detriment of urgent personal considerations. Not surprisingly, then, the New England practice of allowing soldiers to elect their own officers was anathema to the commander in chief, and Washington subsequently made every effort to eliminate such elections since, he said, "the principal objects of their [the officers'] attention" seemed to be "to curry favor with the men."[10]

On November 10, 1775, the Virginian outlined to Col. William Woodford his ideas on military leadership: "... be strict in your discipline; that is, to require nothing unreasonable of your officers and men, but see that whatever is required be punctually complied with. Reward and punish every man according to his merit, without partiality or prejudice; hear his complaints; if well founded, redress them; if otherwise, discourage them, in order to prevent frivolous ones. Discourage vice in every shape...."[11] There is nothing very remarkable in the statement. After all, the Age of Enlightenment frowned upon the barbarous punishments employed in most armies at the time. If Washington advocated that soldiers be treated fairly, be acknowledged as human beings, so did John Burgoyne and Lord Cornwallis in the British army.

At the same time, the Americans wrought no revolution in military training or tactics; they did not seek to stage a guerrilla conflict, did not, so to speak, throw away the book. Actually, there was a mad scramble everywhere in 1775 to secure the standard, up-to-date European treatises on the conduct of war. The conventionality of this literature—much of it reprinted in the colonies—is suggested by a mere reading of the military titles in Charles Evans' *American Bibliography*. Americans' respect for orthodox warfare is underscored by their employment of dozens of European officers in the Continental service, beginning in 1775 with the appointment of three ex-British veterans as generals: Charles Lee, Horatio Gates, and Richard Montgomery. Ironically, however, it was Charles Lee, not George Washington, the former frontier fighter, who in time came to advocate a war of guerrilla bands drawn from irregular forces; it was the Virginian who continued to pin his hopes on a professional army of long-service volunteers.

Nor do we find any distinctive American contribution to organized professional warfare. There were no military writers on the patriot side who were counterparts to the political essayists, to the Jeffersons, Wilsons, Adamses, and so on. One sees no parallel to what transpired in Prussia in the late stages of the Napoleonic era, when reformers such as Gneisenau and Scharnhorst imposed unusually high standards for officers and created division schools of military education and, above them, an unprecedented institution, the War Academy. From the academy came the first modern analytical studies of conflict, highlighted by Karl von Clausewitz's *On War*. In contrast, the United States Military Academy was not founded until 1802, and its graduates were scarcely guaranteed preferential treatment; only one, in fact, rose to the rank of general before 1861. Even so, West Point graduates like Dennis Mahan and Henry Halleck took the lead in setting standards for officer training in the 19th century, and they saw little if anything to emulate in the American officer corps of the Revolution. According to Halleck, the country had survived at critical times such as Valley Forge only because of the exertions of Steuben and other foreign journeymen.[12]

One must ask if American military leadership was all that bad. In truth, it is hard to generalize about it. During the war Congress commissioned 29 major generals, of whom seven resigned, six died, one committed treason, and one was discharged.[13] Forty-four were made brigadier generals and were not advanced beyond that rank. If we assembled a vast amount of biographical data on all of them and ran it through a computer, we might get an average profile. But would such a measurement be very meaningful? Unless we eliminated the former British veterans and the continental European soldiers of fortune, we could hardly gain a distinctive image of the general officers who were American-born or who lived a substantial portion of their lives in the colonies before Lexington and Concord. It is obvious, though, as Halleck said, that the colonists were men of relatively little formal military experience; one need not resort to mathematical computations to find that out. And for virtually every man elevated to the general-officer level in 1775, there were as many or more in the colonies who had comparable backgrounds in warfare. Washington, with a more active war record than most of his colleagues in arms, had only served on the frontier in the French and Indian conflict. And there is no evidence that he had continued his military reading after his retirement in 1758. Nathanael Greene, on the other hand, was an avid student of warfare; but he could boast of no real military participation before the Revolution. As his most recent biographer says, "Greene literally appeared out of nowhere.... He went from the rank of private in the Kentish Guards to that of brigadier general in the Continental army in less than two months."[14]

The story of Greene, by far Washington's most able and successful subordinate, offers us a reminder that there are no absolute criteria for predicting military attainments. It recalls Napoleon's dictum that every man in the ranks carries a marshal's baton in his knapsack, a statement which was almost literally true in his own army in regard to Jourdan and Soult. In fact, neither age nor experience is an absolute indicator. Hannibal, Alexander, Wolfe, Wellington, and Napoleon grasped fame at relatively early ages. Caesar and Cromwell were over 40 when they began their serious soldiering, as was Washington. Turenne's best campaign occurred when he was 63, and Moltke proved himself at 66.

None of these was a great captain simply because he mastered the art of warfare in his time. By such a yardstick, well-grounded British generals like Howe, Burgoyne, Clinton, and Cornwallis should have excelled against the Continental army. Even American generals, with their extremely amateurish backgrounds, were not at so serious a disadvantage as they might have been in a subsequent period of history. For we have noted that British and other European commanders were not specialists in the modern sense, that exacting training was not yet a compelling requirement. American officers who had fought with the British army in the French and Indian War, observing its procedures and reading the standard military treatises like Humphrye Bland's, found in the Revolution that the pattern of warfare as practiced by the so-called experts had hardly changed at all. Granted that Washington and his lieutenants lacked experience in directing massive formations and planning campaigns, but for that matter, British generals—and admirals too—had themselves been subordinate officers in the last war with France. And since then most of them had spent minimal time in the field or on ship. Amazing as it may seem, it is said that Admiral Howe had not been to sea a single time between the wars, that Admiral Keppel, appointed to head the channel fleet in 1778, had not been before the mast in 15 years, and that his successor in 1779, Sir Charles Hardy, had not been on ship in nearly 20 years.

★ ★ ★

From all that has been said, are we to conclude that there was nothing distinctive about American military leadership in the Revolution? On the contrary, I believe there was. For one, the concept of an officer corps reserved for gentlemen or the better sort was never reached, nor was there any real possibility of attaining it with such a consuming demand for officers in a fluid, legally unstructured society. A typical complaint was registered in 1777 to Washington by Col. Henry Beekman Livingston; he reported that he simply could not recruit for his regiment a sufficient complement of officers who bore the character of gentlemen. As a solution, he asked permission to enlist "gentlemen adventurers" from Canada. Interestingly, given a choice between foreigners of social status and Americans lacking class standing, Washington opted for his native countrymen, for the latter, whatever their deficiencies, possessed individual loyalty to the country and a personal stake in the conflict that outsiders lacked.

Moreover, Washington was overwhelmed by the avalanche of foreigners sent over from Europe by the American diplomat Silas Deane. Although there were pleasing exceptions, all too often the Europeans proved to be of marginal competence and displayed a desire for high rank and easy living instead of a concern for the cause and a willingness to undergo personal sacrifices.

There was taking place in America a democratization of military office-holding somewhat analogous to the democratization of politics—recently detailed by Jackson T. Main, Gordon Wood, and James Kirby Martin—as new men were elected to the legislatures and as new offices were thrown open to the public by being made elective rather than appointive.

Perhaps the career of no single American officer better illustrates what the Revolution could do to alter the status of persons than that of Gen. Daniel Morgan. A product of the Virginia frontier, Morgan as a young man was about as wild as frontiersmen in folklore and legend are alleged to have been. He did it all—drinking, gambling, brawling, living with a woman out of wedlock. He was not infrequently in court for nonpayment of debt and assault and battery. But in time he settled down, buying a farm and becoming a responsible citizen. He posted bond for certain county officials, performed jury duty, became a captain in the militia and an overseer of a country road. A veteran of at least two Indian wars, he was skilled in backwoods fighting, particularly the use of the so-called Pennsylvania rifle. Appointed a captain in the Continental army in 1775, he fought at Quebec and Saratoga, with Washington in the Middle Department, and later with Gates, Greene, and Lafayette in the South. In 1780 Congress elected him a brigadier general. Considered an authority on light infantry and partisan-type operations, he was, with the possible exception of Benedict Arnold, the best combat or battlefield officer in the American army. And he advanced on merit alone, for influential ties and family station were nonexistent.

Even so, he came to view himself as a gentleman, ever conscious of his dignity and honor. Instead of thinking himself lucky to be an officer at all in light of his social background, he desired to climb ever higher. In 1779, when a newly created light unit went to Anthony Wayne, Morgan was bitterly disappointed. "I cannot therefore but feel deeply effected with this injury done my reputation," he informed Congress, and he temporarily withdrew from active duty with the army.[15]

Let us at this point raise a question for which there may be no ready answer, or which should be referred to the trained student of psychohistory: namely, is a man's perception of himself, particularly of his niche in society, changed by the office or position to which he is elevated? A British official, interrogating Americans captured at Quebec, was amazed to find that the officers were mechanics, farmers, and tradesmen who, nevertheless, insisted they be extended the courtesy due gentlemen. I suspect that such a change did occur for many officers of modest backgrounds, and that the mental transformation is less difficult to make in societies that are somewhat open and fluid.

Then, too, there is a related question equally incapable of satisfactory analysis with the historian's traditional tools. Does the putting on of ribbons or epaulets immediately result in the creation of what has been termed a military mentality? If so, at times at least, does the generalization apply to these American amateurs, men with little in the way of even meaningful militia experience, many of whom—like Morgan—were from very common human stock? Countless officers left the service because of low pay and other hardships, but so did dozens more because they were denied advancement and other forms of recognition to which military men have been extremely sensitive.

Repeatedly Washington pictured the spirit of discontent among his subordinates as "truly alarming," particularly in the Virginia line, where it raged "like an epidemical disease."[16] John Adams complained of being "wearied to Death with the Wrangles between military officers, high and low. They Quarrell like Cats and Dogs. They worry one another like Mastiffs, Scrambling for Rank and Pay like Apes for Nuts."[17]

Or, we may inquire, is all of this only thé civilian coming out in the soldier, the citizen conscious of his worth and free to do something about it, at liberty to complain without fear of serious recrimination and, should this recourse fail, to resign from the service? As Washington explained to Lafayette following a particularly embarrassing outburst from Gen. John Sullivan, "in a free and republican Government, you cannot restrain the voice of the multitude;" here "every Man will speak as he thinks."[18]

Now it is not beyond the realm of possibility that there remains another reason why officers thirsted for accolades. It may have been owing to the very seamlessness of American society, for the ways that men were recognized in more rigidly hierarchical social systems were absent in America. One gets a hint of a desire for this kind of limelight even before the Revolution in the frequent references to men by their militia titles, and not simply when an officer was on active duty during an Indian contest or an Anglo-French war. Reference by title seems to have been the manner of addressing many if not most of them in daily life, or so one gathers from the court records, the land patents, the legislative journals, the newspapers, and so on. Virginia, remarked a visitor, must surely be a retreat for heroes, for he seldom met a man who was not a captain or a colonel. And in New England, according to Norman H. Dawes, "military titles were employed more meticulously than any other forms of deferential address."[19]

Other suggestions come to mind at this point, perhaps leading still further beyond the confines of prudence. What may be made of the number of Americans who successfully sought British military commissions before the Revolution—Apthrop, Butler, Byrd, De Lancey, De Peyster, Lyman, Schuyler, among others? To the list one could have added the name of George Washington had he been able to obtain the commission he sought, the same Washington who ordered for his home at Mount Vernon busts of great European military commanders. All of these cases might total up to evidence of a desire for a form of recognition unavailable in colonial society.

Such a framework, I would speculate, gives deeper meaning to the discontent of the Revolutionary officers that culminated in the Newburgh Addresses in 1783, a subject of no small interest to historians.[20] The evidence, as I read it, does not necessarily justify the conclusion that a full-fledged conspiracy existed, though there were no doubt a handful of would-be conspirators in the cantonment on the Hudson. In any case, there is no doubt that the officers had genuine grievances and concerns over back salaries and the need for some form of postwar compensation for their services and sacrifices. (Congress finally voted them full salaries for a period of five years.) But could they not better face the plainness of civilian life with a public commendation in the form of deserved emoluments? The transition might be eased, additionally, by participation in the Society of the Cincinnati, an organization which, despite the denunciations of its critics, scarcely appears to have been designed to create and perpetuate a military aristocracy.

To find some things about the warrior's life appealing—the comradeship, the esprit de corps, the applause of one's countrymen for performing heroic deeds—is not to be a janissary or a praetorian. If there was an ambivalence among the officers about things military, it was probably no more pronounced than that among the public at large. A German traveler in the Confederation period, Johann Schoepf, observed that a "liking for military show is everywhere a temptation, but in America and among Americans is all the more surprising, since there they profess on all occasions a hatred for soldiers, or wish to appear as if they hated them."[21]

When all is said, one still gets the feeling that the Continental officers were more civilians than soldiers, that their dedication to republican principles was as strong as that of most political leaders. In fact, they often said so. Any definition of republicanism—admittedly an imprecise term at that time—included a concern for the public good, for the practice of virtue and the notion of sacrifice. And yet the officers, carrying such principles into daily practice, looked around them and saw far too much "idleness and dissipation" in the cities, an inordinate desire for profits and riches on the part of hordes of merchants and farmers. Washington lashed out at the "infamous practices of speculators, monopolizers, and all that class of gentry which are preying upon our very vitals, and, for the sake of a little dirty pelf, are putting the rights and liberties of the country into the most imminent danger...."[22] There was likewise a concern that Congressmen themselves were not making ample sacrifices when the composition of the lawmaking body changed greatly from year to year, at least partly—if one can judge from certain political leaders' complaints—because of a desire to avoid the sacrifices involved in being away from home.

In contrast, men like Gen. Alexander McDougall stayed in the field, although the New York officer pointed out in 1780 that the generals had not received an increase in their pay or maintenance allowance since the beginning of the war. Two years later McDougall reported that he had received his salary only twice during the war. Newburgh was only the last—and most serious—episode in the officers' long campaign for equitable treatment from Congress and the states.

Quite obviously, the officers had become politicized in defense of their own interests. But they had scarcely been apolitical at any time; they had had their champions in Congress whom they courted assiduously—the names of Schuyler, Gates, and Lee come quickly to mind.

Here was an army whose leadership was anything but divorced from society. Was its political sensitivity mainly a negative factor, a cause only for wrangling within its own ranks and with Congress? Our observations thus far would seemingly elicit such a singular conclusion. There is, however, another aspect of the army's political side and its civilian background. And it leads to a discussion of what I consider to be the most significant part of American military leadership in the Revolution. At a level other than that of securing their individual and collective recognition and rewards, the most successful ranking officers displayed a crucial political awareness. To provide for their armies, they needed great tact and diplomacy in a variety of areas. These qualities were called for in dealing with Congress, the states, the civilian population, the militia, and, of course, the officers and men of the Continental army.

The demands were enormous. "A general of an American Army must be everything; and that is being more than one man can long sustain,"[23] complained Horatio Gates in the midst of the Saratoga campaign. Gates' remark squares with what I think was a sine qua non of the war. Simply put, an army had to survive—to be an object of concern to British commanders, a source of intimidation for the loyalists, a rallying point for the militia, and a living, day-to-day symbol of the Revolution and emerging American nationality. This point about survival takes on an added dimension in view of the studies of Eric Robson, Piers Mackesy, and others who have raised serious doubts whether Britain ever had a good opportunity to win the Revolutionary War, whether it was not such an unprecedented war in terms of its arduous requirements in logistics, strategy, communication, and coordination as to all but exclude that possibility.

To exist, then, was almost to guarantee that Britain could not prevail. But was survival all that easy? Even if human resources were in abundance, even if the Revolution was a people's war, a countryside in arms, I still think not, and for the reasons implicit in Horatio Gates' observation. But before we assess more closely the matter of survival, of keeping relatively effective Continental armies in the field, we should first underscore how different in many respects have been the responsibilities of generalship in recent times. The general of the 20th century has often had to deal only with his immediate superior in the army, with a civilian department head, and perhaps, in the United States at least, with the President in the role of commander in chief. His field army is likely to be ready made—already trained, accoutred, and provisioned when it arrives in the combat zone and prepares for battle. For an American general, contacts with the civilian population at home have been minimal or nonexistent. Neither desertions nor expiring enlistments have been likely to hamper or alter his campaign plans. Whatever his problems—and they are not to be minimized—they have been at variance with those of American generals of the Revolution.

What was an American army of the War of Independence? First and foremost, it was an agglomerate. Baron von Closen of the French forces marveled to see troops "of every age, even of children of fifteen, of whites and blacks, almost naked, unpaid, and rather poorly fed...."[24] Eventually, the army consisted of one-year and three-year regulars; of militia units, at times assigned to Continental service for a fixed period but more likely not, subject only to the whim and caprice of officers and men; of short-term volunteers; and of roving partisan bands, which were not always part of any formal military structure. Within the army men came and went, their numbers invariably declining late in the year, as terms of duty ended, or when seasonal demands for agricultural labor drew farmers back to the land. Desertion was a serious problem, more so than we probably realize: a recent investigator asserts that a quarter of all the Continentals took unauthorized leave at some time.[25]

Obstacles similar to those that confronted Washington when he initially took command of the army in 1775 were subsequently encountered by every field commander during each year of the war. For Washington it meant creating order out of confusion—exacting a precise count of men, muskets, tents, and clothing; instilling discipline in the independent-minded New England husbandmen and the companies of newly arrived, high-spirited backwoods riflemen from Virginia, Maryland, and Pennsylvania; and easing rivalries in this peculiar coalition war, where jealousies were not restricted to contentions between Yankees and southerners over the respective merits of muskets and rifles but extended to Connecticut's wanting no Massachusetts men in its regiments and to the Bay Colony's displeasure over mixing Rhode Islanders with its own troops.

How did one hold an army together, particularly in light of the annual year-end trauma? By a mixture of threats, cajolery, and artful persuasion, by improving conditions in the service, and by explaining the issues of a struggle being fought for freedom rather than for the customary reasons of territorial gain or dynastic rivalry. It is revealing and instructive to read the general orders of American commanders, particularly Washington's, for one finds that the patriot military leaders did much to spread what Washington described as enlightened thinking. They were in a real sense teachers, explaining in everyday language ideas that the common soldier might not have understood fully from a reading of *Common Sense* and the Declaration of Independence.

Time and again there were scenes of drama. Witness Richard Montgomery before the gates of Quebec begging his New Englanders for a few more precious days. Witness Washington in search of reenlistments, addressing each regiment during a critical moment in the Trenton-Princeton campaign. Witness Daniel Morgan making the rounds of the campfires the night before Cowpens, steeling the backs of his shaky militiamen with promises of glory *and* personal safety. Witness Nathanael Greene with the haughty guerrilla chieftain Thomas Sumter, whose upcountry forces he wished to coordinate with his own southern army. "You may strike a hundred strokes and reap little benefit from them," he counseled the South Carolinian, "unless you have a good Army to take advantage of your success."[26]

To sustain an army, to drum up new regiments every spring while enticing the much-abused militia to hold the lines in the interim months, to procure sufficient provisions, uniforms, tents, guns, and ammunition— all this entailed endless appeals to civilian leaders not only in Congress but at the state and local levels as well. That the generals carried on a continuous correspondence with the lawmakers in Philadelphia is common knowledge, and we need not be reminded that Congress, for a variety of reasons, was more often than not incapable of rising to the occasion. Not so widely realized—and it should be stressed—is the fact that the generals' letterbooks bulged with copies of epistles imploring state chief executives to have their legislatures make up for congressional deficiencies. Nor were county courts and town governing agencies ignored. In fact, an American general was a scavenger: he had to claw and scrape to keep the odds and ends that he designated an army in one piece. He was often a cheerleader as well, not only for his tattered legions but for the homefront element too. "We must not despair," wrote Washington to Gov. John Mathews. "I trust the experience of error will enable us to act better in future. A cloud may yet pass over us, individuals may be ruined; and the Country at large, or particular States, undergo temporary distress; but certain I am, that it is in our power to bring the War to a happy conclusion."[27]

If all else failed, a general might resort to impressment of desperately needed goods and supplies, forage, and wagons, but he did so at the risk of violent repercussions from state politicians. Besides, as Washington admitted, the practice bred—even among tested veterans—"a disposition to licentiousness, plunder, and Robbery."[28] For the same practical reasons, generals usually turned over local inhabitants discovered trading with the enemy to civil magistrates.[29] At times, with no evident alternative, a general might enforce statutory law, as did Gen. Alexander McDougall in the New York highlands, but he deplored the necessity of doing the work of state officials, who could at any moment scream of military interference. Indeed, both New Jersey and Pennsylvania lodged repeated protests over the army's usurping civil control, the former state going so far as to temporarily place a tax on Continental quartermasters operating within its borders.

In still other ways danger lurked behind the lines in the form of civilian pressures. Although Congress only infrequently dabbled in strategy, most notably in relation to Canada and in the campaign around New York City in 1776, that assemblage did want the army to fight. Moreover, individual congressmen, governors, state legislators, and additional noncombatants peppered Washington and his lieutenants in the various theaters with a barrage of advice.[30] (One is reminded of Gen. George C. Marshall's wry comment that he learned quite early in World War II that the politicians demanded some form of offensive every year.) Not every correspondent wrote from disinterested patriotism, as when, for example, Gov. John Rutledge of South Carolina slyly confided to Daniel Morgan that a strike at British-held Ninety-Six would incidentally provide the Americans with an opportunity to carry the governor's own slaves away from that post.

★   ★   ★

American generals, civilian in background, were asked to fight a war that was civilian in style. They were pushed and pulled, pressured and coerced, inadequately supported and not infrequently maligned. Some fell from grace because of political and sectional factors, others because of undue civilian interference combined with their own mistakes, and still others, of course, because of their incompetence. Congress never really trusted Philip Schuyler after the ill-fated Canadian invasion of 1775–76, an almost hopeless assignment from the beginning. Later the lawmakers used his army's evacuation of Fort Ticonderoga—actually a wise move—as one of several reasons for replacing him in the Northern Department. But it was the South that became the graveyard of American commanders—first Robert Howe, after the loss of Georgia and after South Carolinians failed to give him their full backing (and after he fought a duel with Christopher Gadsden); next Benjamin Lincoln, after his surrender of Charleston, a city Gadsden and the Carolinians had angrily insisted he defend until it was too late to escape; and finally Horatio Gates, who responded to—among other things— the urging of North Carolina leaders that he take the offensive in what was to result in disaster at Camden.

To take a heterogeneous throng, somehow wire it together, and make it fight and at least occasionally win, all without antagonizing civilians and public officials, these were the challenges to generalship in Revolutionary America. It is scarcely a wonder that, by such criteria, only two commanders achieved preeminence, Washington and Greene, although a handful more scored modest successes. Yet it was their civilian backgrounds that enabled them to understand what was needed and how to go about attaining it, frustrating though their circumstances might be. This conflict would not be the last American war to be shaped by politics and civilian demands. Perhaps it has been a high price to pay when military men have often felt that they were being exploited or hamstrung in their efforts, but it has been one the American people have insisted on. And the most perceptive American military leaders have recognized the rules of the game from Washington's time forward.

Whatever the theory of civil-military relations, whatever the tensions between politicians and soldiers in the Revolution, both groups recognized, tacitly anyway, that the Continentals had to perform an assortment of political functions: to aid local constabularies against the loyalists, to protect lives and property of citizens, to combat inflation and profiteering and counterfeiting, and to sustain civil government—in the case of Nathanael Greene, to the point of assisting South Carolinians in convening their first assembly in many months and in Georgia literally reviving the state's shattered political institutions.[31] Hence, another dimension to the manifold nature of military leadership in the War of Independence.

When was there no longer a need for military leadership? It came with the end of the struggle, with the treaty of peace. The generals were ready to relinquish power, to shape their swords into ploughshares, perhaps as eagerly as Congress wished them to do so. Ironically, it was not the generals—those who had over the years accumulated the most serious grievances, had suffered most at the hands of civil authority—that were involved in the still mysterious and controversial Newburgh episode. Even the more hotheaded senior officers such as McDougall and Knox wanted no part of the matter. The conspirators—if that is what they were—came from the ranks of the junior officers. The firebrand John Armstrong, Jr., author of the Newburgh Addresses, was 24, and Lewis Nicola, who supposedly suggested a crown to Washington, was a colonel, not a general.

Lacking—as we have already stressed—social cohesion, lacking too the need for postwar existence, the officer phalanx never engaged in the continual self-examination that characterized the Prussian officer corps, which after Jena began redefining with each succeeding generation its outlook on the nature and purpose of its role in a changing world. The American officer cadre had no further part to play in the process of postwar nation-building.

Despite the vicissitudes of the 1780's as the union was gradually settling to firmer foundations, there was no wholesale anarchy and no crisis of legitimacy. If there were a cluster of lesser officers who shared the forebodings of Colonel Nicola, they never had the opportunity to become caudillos, to tred the path of Bolívar's lieutenants that led to military domination in Latin America. Nor did the military element have a bureaucratic function to perform, as has been true in some new underdeveloped nations since 1945. There the armies—with their officers graduates of Sandhurst or St. Cyr, Oxford or the Sorbonne—have been almost alone in their administrative and managerial know-how. In America, the Continental army was not what David Rapoport has seen the military establishment to be in the so-called Third World of our time, that is, "a national school where the citizens can learn appropriate civic virtues and important technical and administrative skills that may contribute to the maintenance and/or improvement of their community." [32]

America was not wanting for men of learning and training in statecraft, for those committed to republican virtue. All the same, the officers, as individuals rather than collectively, returned to their respective states, where they engaged in various forms of public service as civilians, where their Revolutionary experiences were brought to bear on the problems of building a more durable American union. One recalls Albert J. Beveridge's observation that Capt. John Marshall's winter at Valley Forge gave the future jurist a greater insight into the needs of national government than any political or legal tract he ever read.

Notwithstanding times of trial, stress, and even personal risk in the civil-military sector, the Revolutionary generation escaped what Morris Janowitz has described as the great danger that armies pose to free societies, when "the military profession comes to be seen as a distinct and separate establishment by civilian society and in turn...begins to see itself as alienated from civilian society."[33]

Notes

[1] Karl von Clausewitz, *On War,* trans. J. J. Graham, 3 vols. (New York: Barnes and Noble, 1940), 1:12–13, 3:121–31. There is a vast literature on the subject of leadership. Undoubtedly the best bibliography available is Ralph M. Stogdill's *Handbook of Leadership: A Survey of Theory and Research* (New York: Free Press, 1974), which abstracts and analyzes more than 3,000 books and articles.

[2] Maurice de Saxe, *My Reveries Upon the Art of War,* trans. T. R. Phillips, in *Roots of Strategy: A Collection of Military Classics* (Harrisburg, Pa.: Military Service Publishing Co., 1955), p. 297.

[3] Karl Demeter, *The German Officer-Corps in Society and State, 1650–1945* (New York: Frederick A. Praeger, 1965), p. 68. In 1711 Joseph Addison spoke of the "three great professions" of "divinity, law, and physic." Quoted in A. M. Carr-Saunders, "Professionalization in Historical Perspective," in *Professionalization,* ed. Howard M. Vollmer and Donald L. Mills (Englewood Cliffs, N.J.: Prentice-Hall, 1966), p. 3.

[4] Peter Paret, *Yorck and the Era of Prussian Reform, 1807–1815* (Princeton: Princeton University Press, 1966), p. 111.

[5] M. S. Anderson, *Europe in the Eighteenth Century, 1713–1783* (New York: Holt, Rinehart and Winston, 1961), p. 141.

[6] Émile G. Léonard, *L'Armée et ses Problèmes au XVIIIe siècle* (Paris: Plon, 1958), p. 175.

[7] William B. Willcox, *Portrait of a General: Sir Henry Clinton in the War of Independence* (New York: Alfred A. Knopf, 1964), p. 14. See also James Hayes, "The Royal House of Hanover and the British Army, 1714–1760," *Bulletin of the John Rylands Library* 40 (March 1958):328–57.

[8] Franklin and Mary Wickwire, *Cornwallis: The American Adventure* (Boston: Houghton Mifflin, 1970), p. 9.

[9] A good exposition of this point is in Lynn L. Marshall's "The Strange Stillbirth of the Whig Party," *American Historical Review* 72 (January 1967):456–57.

[10] George Washington, *The Writings of George Washington,* ed. John C. Fitzpatrick, 39 vols. (Washington: U.S. Government Printing Office, 1931–44), 3:450–51. For examples of other statements, see ibid., 7:309–10, 475, 9:68–69, 10:26.

[11] Ibid., 4:80.

[12] Henry W. Halleck, *Elements of Military Art and Science*, 3d ed. (New York, London: D. Appleton & Co., 1863), pp. 379–408, 445–46.

[13] The total of 29 excludes those officers given brevet rank in 1783.

[14] Theodore Thayer, "Nathanael Greene: Revolutionary War Strategist," in George A. Billias, ed., *George Washington's Generals* (New York: William Morrow, 1964), pp. 110–11. British overconfidence in the War of Independence stemmed in part from what Burgoyne called the absence among Americans of "men of military science." Edward B. de Fonblanque, ... *Life and Correspondence of John Burgoyne, General, Statesman, Dramatist* (London: Macmillan, 1876), p. 484.

James Alcock, announcing the opening of a military school in Annapolis, declared, "there appears at this time a great alacrity amongst all ranks of people to perfect themselves in the Military Art." *Maryland Journal*, September 6, 1775.

[15] Don Higginbotham, *Daniel Morgan: Revolutionary Rifleman* (Chapel Hill: University of North Carolina Press, 1961), p. 97.

[16] Washington, *Writings*, 11:180.

[17] L. H. Butterfield, ed., *Adams Family Correspondence*, vol. 2 (Cambridge: Belknap Press of Harvard University Press, 1963), p. 245. A similar complaint appears in the *Maryland Gazette*, February 13, 1777.

[18] Washington, *Writings*, 12:383.

[19] Norman H. Dawes, "Titles as Symbols of Prestige in Seventeenth Century New England," *William and Mary Quarterly*, 3d ser. 6 (January 1949):69–83, especially 78–79. Prof. Mary Beth Norton informs me that the expression "rattlesnake colonel" was used in Virginia, where titles were eagerly sought and evidently easily obtained— all one needed to do to be designated a colonel was to kill a rattlesnake! See also Marcus Cunliffe, *Soldiers and Civilians: The Martial Spirit in America, 1775–1865* (Boston: Little, Brown, 1968), pp. 74, 447 n9.

[20] The *William and Mary Quarterly* has published a total of three articles on Newburgh just within the last four years: Richard H. Kohn, "The Inside History of the Newburgh Conspiracy: America and the Coup d'Etat," 3d ser. 27 (April 1970):187– 220; Paul David Nelson, "Horatio Gates at Newburgh, 1783: A Misunderstood Role. With a Rebuttal by Richard H. Kohn," ibid. 29 (January 1972):143–58; C. Edward Skeen, "The Newburgh Conspiracy Reconsidered. With a Rebuttal by Richard H. Kohn," ibid. 31 (April 1974):273–98.

[21] Johann David Schoepf, *Travels in the Confederation*, trans. and ed. Alfred J. Morrison, 2 vols. (1911; reprint ed., New York: Bergman Publishers, 1968), 2:206–7. But if men relished military titles, why did the public accommodate them, in view of the antiprofessional attitudes so prevalent in the colonies and later in the independent nation? Perhaps in some measure because of the importance that Americans placed upon protection at the time. John Shy calls the 17th and 18th centuries an "age of survival." He argues that "military 'survival,' at least in a political if not a physical sense, was an important question for American society even to the end of the War of 1812." Shy, "The American Military Experience: History and Learning," *Journal of Interdisciplinary History* 1 (Winter 1971):205–28.

22 Washington, *Writings,* 15:180.

23 Gates to Elizabeth Gates, September 22, 1777, Gates Papers, New-York Historical Society.

24 Baron Ludwig von Closen, *Revolutionary Journal, 1780–1783,* ed. Evelyn M. Acomb (Chapel Hill: Published for the Institute of Early American History and Culture at Williamsburg, Va., by the University of North Carolina Press, 1958), p. 102.

25 James H. Edmonson, "Desertion in the American Army During the Revolutionary War," (Ph.D. diss., Louisiana State University, 1971).

26 Greene to Sumter, January 8, 1781, Sumter Papers, Library of Congress.

27 Washington, *Writings,* 22:176. It may have been unusual, but there were moments when state legislatures responded quickly and fully. See the excellent document and editorial note on Virginia's acting to clothe the state's troops in 1777. George Mason, *The Papers of George Mason, 1725–1792,* ed. Robert A. Rutland, 3 vols. (Chapel Hill: University of North Carolina Press, 1970), 1:355–57.

28 Washington, *Writings,* 10:253–54.

29 Ibid., 11:420, 12:497, 13:18.

30 A good example is Robert R. Livingston, who conceded to Washington that he offered advice "pretty freely." George Dangerfield, *Chancellor Robert R. Livingston of New York, 1746–1813* (New York: Harcourt, Brace, 1960), pp. 85–86. For Congress, see Jonathan G. Rossie, "The Politics of Command: The Continental Congress and Its Generals," (Ph.D. diss., University of Wisconsin, 1966).

31 I have enlarged upon Greene's political role in *The War of American Independence: Military Attitudes, Policies, and Practice, 1763–1789* (New York: Macmillan, 1971), pp. 375–76.

32 David C. Rapoport, "A Comparative Theory of Military and Political Types," in *Changing Patterns of Military Politics,* ed. Samuel P. Huntington (New York: Free Press of Glencoe, 1962), p. 71.

33 Morris Janowitz, "The Emergent Military," in *Public Opinion and the Military Establishment,* ed. Charles C. Moskos, Jr. (Beverly Hills, Calif.: Sage Publications, 1971), p. 260.

DON HIGGINBOTHAM received A.B. and M.A. degrees from Washington University and a Ph.D. degree from Duke University. Currently a professor of history at the University of North Carolina, Chapel Hill, he has taught previously at Duke University, the College of William and Mary, Longwood College, and Louisiana State University. His publications include *Daniel Morgan: Revolutionary Rifleman* (1961), *The War of American Independence* (1971), and various articles and essays. In addition, he has edited volume 1 of *The Papers of James Iredell* (1974) and, with Kenneth Nebenzahl, *An Atlas of the American Revolution* (1974).

The late Sir Lewis Namier observed that "the great historian is like the great artist or doctor: after he has done his work, others should not be able to practice within its sphere in the terms of the preceding era." Namier was of course not speaking of himself, but the remark applies well to his career and its consequences. And it was he more than any other individual who made Freudian psychology respectable as an implement to be used by the historian and the biographer.

With Namier's authority and example before them, even the conservatives among us can no longer tell the psychohistorians to stop their pother and go away. Traditionalists may still believe that a historical writer, if he is a man of wisdom, stands the best chance of arriving at greater understanding through the discovery of new evidence or a more skillful reading of the old evidence. Yet every thoughtful person among us—and what is a historian if not thoughtful?—recognizes that modern psychology, including the Freudian version, has vastly enlarged our understanding of ourselves by revealing the intertwinings of conscious and subconscious motives.

How far can such delicate and difficult examinations of motives be applied to historical personages, whose only testimony is what happens to survive among what they happened to record about themselves? Professor Bruce Mazlish of the Massachusetts Institute of Technology defines some of the terms, describes the procedures and problems, and then illustrates the psychohistorian's approach in a few pages devoted specifically to George Washington that will raise some eyebrows. (Query: Can figures of speech supply the evidence not found in documents?)

Despite the esoteric language required by his method, Professor Mazlish proceeds with ease and urbanity, for his professional career has been spent in the large borderland between history and psychology, and he has moved back and forth between the two domains, which he considers essentially one, as readily as he has moved between national cultures and historical epochs.

Leadership in the
American Revolution
The Psychological Dimension

BRUCE MAZLISH

In thinking of my role at this symposium, two terms keep occurring to me: *interloper* and *intermediary*. The first, according to the *American Heritage Dictionary,* is one who violates the "legally established trading rights of others"; the second is "one that acts as an agent between persons or things; a means." I hope that I shall be the second, and not the first, but I cannot give you surety for this. Thus, I cannot speak to you as a "legally established" American historian, in the sense of this being my major field, but only as a historian concerned with the comparative history of revolutions and with the general psychological dimensions of history. I hope that this state of affairs will not lead me to violate the study of the American Revolution but will rather permit me to act as a go-between for it and other studies. If nothing else, in seeking to supply an outsider's comparative and psychological perspective I may serve the happy function of confirming you in the belief that nothing is to be gained from such an effort, or else that you must seek other trade partners.

What makes the matter most hazardous is my own definition of psychohistory, in which the "history" is at least as important as the "psycho." In earlier, more confident days, psychoanalysts could parachute into the historical field, do a fairly quick psychobiography, secure in the belief that intrapsychic processes were relatively insulated from external historical factors, and emerge triumphantly with the scalps, if not the heads, of their famous subjects, need I say, now nicely "shrunk." Alas, ego-psychological developments and Erikson have destroyed such halcyon possibilities. One needs now to know as much about the political, social, economic, and intellectual conflicts of the time as about the Oedipal conflicts of the individual. As a result, in spite of all my efforts to read up on the American Revolution, I must confess to being one of the last of the amateurs.

My apologies are over—I shall now interlope and intermediate. In discussing the psychological dimension of leadership in the American revolution, the first problem is to identify the leaders. As an outsider and comparativist, I was first struck by the absence of what I shall call "elite" studies. Objective statistical analyses of the kind done, say, in the Hoover Institute studies of Communist or Nazi leadership cadres seem to be missing in the American field, as do Lasswellian-type analyses of political agitators, administrators, and propagandists. Dankwart A. Rustow's brilliant review-essay "The Study of Elites," published in *World Politics,* mentions books on the Turkish and Ceylonese elites, but there is nothing remotely comparable on Americans.[1]

Now I am not saying that there are no studies of American leaders in the Revolutionary period which use data on education, economic standing, literacy, social background, etc. As far as I can see, there is a plethora of these. It is simply that for better or for worse—it may indeed be for better, as a glance at Rustow's article may show—they are not put in the same form as the comparative elite studies that I have in mind. Thus there is no readily available "handbook" offering overall "objective" data on American Revolutionary leadership.[2]

It may be that a democratic revolution does not sit readily with elite studies (it is doubtful if the Communist revolutionaries analyze themselves in these terms, either). Or more likely, that the concept of the elite as a social classification emerges only after a society based on orders and ranks breaks into class and elite stratifications as the result of a revolution such as that of 1776 or 1789. Or most likely of all, that one can only effectively do elite studies where there is a nationwide party, as with the Communists or Nazis, or a national parliament, or at least national politics involved in the revolution.

Thus the absence of conventional behavioristic elite studies, while it complicates our task of identifying the leaders, points attention to the actual factors conditioning the exercise of leadership during the American Revolution. For my own satisfaction at least, I have had to ask what were the political and social contexts in which a potential leader might emerge and what tasks did he face. What follows will seem obvious to you; its only interest will lie in the fact that it is not obvious to someone whose usual concern has been about European and non-Western revolutions.

The most striking fact for me is that the American is an extraordinarily complicated and untidy revolution. It is not a "national" revolution like the English or French, where local and provincial issues, although important, are not paramount. Events in England in 1640 took place in the context of a sovereign Parliament; those in France in 1789, of an Estates General, summoned by the king and in Paris. There is simply no equivalent of parliamentary London or monarchical Paris in America, though there were good-sized cities such as Philadelphia, which ranked among the four or five largest English-speaking cities in the British Empire. Hence, there is no national revolution as in England but a confused series of colonial or provincial ones, with the leaders in 1763 not the same as those in 1776, and no urban revolution as in France, where a Robespierre could emerge as master of the masses.

The overriding demand on an American leader then, was that he be able to work toward unity of effort, if not unification itself. (In fact, the British seemed the foremost leaders in this effort, inadvertently bringing the colonies together by such measures as the Stamp Act.) Yet, such a leader could only exert a unifying influence by working his way up through local leadership and by reflecting colonial interests and slow-paced colonial responses to the need for unity. As Sydnor puts it in his *Gentlemen Freeholders,* "in exercising its vast electoral power the Assembly seldom chose a man who had not served in the Assembly, and it usually chose from its present membership. All of the first ten governors of the State of Virginia, of the seven Virginia signers of the Declaration of Independence, and of the five Virginia delegates to the Federal Constitutional Convention had been members of the Assembly except Edmund Randolph."[3] Thus, most leadership resulted initially from appealing to one's fellow members of the elite. Whatever the correct argument over the role of the mob in the American Revolution, it is clear that leaders were not trying to appeal to them, except in local instances. Not demagoguery but, at most, oratory in a house of burgesses was the skill generally demanded. Addressing a highly literate people of relatively homogeneous race and religion, not consciously divided into class, the leader could earn his way by a well-penned pamphlet or declaration, or even a treatise. While the situation might vary widely—one is struck by the different kinds of leaders and followers in, say, Virginia and Massachusetts, where internal conflict and habits of deference were different—the variation is about a common theme. Gradually, out of planters and lawyers a new generation of leaders emerged, conditioned by the need to slowly espouse independence—no one could be a leader for long who hung back from his followers—and, even more gradually, to press for unity and eventually unification. Only with the emergence of national forums—the Stamp Act Congress first and then the various Continental Congresses—could these new leaders, however, find the appropriate institution within which to function effectively and to exercise the qualities required of them by the structural demands imposed by the forces we have so briefly analyzed.

It is in this context that we can try to talk about the psychological aspect of leadership in the American Revolution. Although we do not have at our disposal an objectively delineated elite, we do have long compendiums of minor local leaders and even a clearly agreed upon group of major leaders: Washington, Jefferson, Madison, John Adams, Samuel Adams, Benjamin Franklin—their names seem to appear on everyone's list. Here, surely, is at least a subjective list, fit material for psychological statements. Can we not generalize from them as to the psychological dimension of leadership in the American Revolution? Well, let us see.

★   ★   ★

The first question to ask is: were the "great leaders," as I shall call them, "charismatic," to use a word bordering on the sociological and the psychological? *Charisma,* as is well known, is a term linked to the name of Max Weber; it is also an extraordinarily ambiguous term. In Weber's sociology, it is one of the three concepts by which to analyze the ways in which authority is legitimized: traditional authority, such as that associated with hereditary monarchs and those others who have always, so to speak, held it; rational-legal authority, obeyed because it is sanctioned by the system of rules under which the leader has won and holds office; and charismatic authority, based on faith in the exceptional personal qualities of the leader. According to Weber, where patterns of traditional and rational-legal authority have broken down, a charismatic situation arises in which authority must be self made. The analysis is complicated by the fact that we also talk about charisma as a personality trait. For clearly, although Weber's first two categories are situational, his last seems to imply a psychological as well as situational demand. Hence we hear people speak, for example, of

Franklin Delano Roosevelt as a charismatic leader when obviously he achieved authority by rational-legal means, although endowed with much personal attractiveness and charm.

Was the situation in America in the 1770's charismatic? It seems to me the answer is no. By and large, the leaders were chosen by rational-legal means, though these were amended so as to eliminate the traditional authority of the king and his appointees. Such a view, incidentally, coincides with the conviction that the American Revolution was not particularly a social revolution, as my readings confirm for me. It follows, almost by default, then, that the leaders of the American Revolution would not be charismatic, and I believe this to be the case. Thus I think that Seymour Martin Lipset is using the wrong terms when he says in *The First New Nation* that "the early American Republic, like many of the new nations, was legitimized by *charisma*. We tend to forget today that, in his time, George Washington was idolized as much as many of the contemporary leaders of new states."[4] So is Franco today idolized in Spain, as was Stalin in the Soviet Union. But neither is to be considered charismatic for that reason. The truth about George Washington and his role is more adequately expressed by an early writer, Henry T. Tuckerman, who in his *Essays, Biographical and Critical* (1857) remarked: "If we may borrow a metaphor from natural philosophy, it was not by magnetism, so much as by gravitation, that [George Washington's] moral authority was established."[5] In short, neither Washington nor any of the other great leaders was a charismatic personality, nor were they even operating in a truly charismatic situation.

There is a second question to be asked, growing out of some research of my own. In my study of various revolutions I became struck with the frequency with which a number of prominent revolutionaries—though not all, by any means—exhibited strong traits of what I have come to call "revolutionary asceticism." As Eric Hobsbawm puts the matter, "There is ... a persistent affinity between revolutions and puritanism. I can think of no well-established organised revolutionary movement or regime which has not developed marked puritanical doctrines.... The libertarian ... component of revolutionary movements, though sometimes strong or even dominant at the actual moment of liberation, has never been able to resist the puritan. The Robespierres always win out over the Dantons."[6] In pursuing this line of thought, I came to combine a notion of Weber's with a notion of Freud's. Weber, of course, had taken the cluster of traits—self-denial, self-discipline, and so forth—associated with the term "ascetic" and traditionally placed in the service of religion and traced their evolution into worldly asceticism, where they were placed in the service of economic, i.e., capitalistic, activity. I have tried to appropriate this idea and to apply it in developing an understanding of how and why asceticism has also come increasingly to be employed in the service of revolutionary activity. Alongside of this idea, however, I have tried to place one of Freud's. In his *Group Psychology and the Analysis of the Ego,* Freud spoke of the leader with "few libidinal ties." Such a leader, as Freud tells us, "loved no one but himself, or other people only in so far as they served his needs. To objects his ego gave away no more than was barely necessary. . . . the members of a group stand in need of the illusion that they are equally and justly loved by their leader; but the leader himself need love no one else, he may be of a masterful nature, absolutely narcissistic, self-confident and independent."[7] This is the sort of leader, in fact, who can deny the normal bonds of friendship, feeling, and affection and eliminate all human considerations in the name of devotion to the revolution. A Robespierre can send his friends Desmoulins and Danton to the guillotine without a shred of compunction. A Lenin can refuse to listen to Beethoven's *Appassionata* sonata because it may weaken his revolutionary fervor. Taken together, the virtual absence of libidinal ties—or more properly expressed, the existence of displaced libido—and the salient presence of traditional ascetic traits make for what I have called the "revolutionary ascetic."

I shall spare you the intimate details of why, psychologically, such character traits are functional for the revolutionary. Even on the purely overt level, one can see that they allow him readily to break ties with the past, with family, and with existing authority, and to do so in the face of threats of poverty, torture, and deprivation of various sorts. His ascetic traits appeal to followers, who seek an obviously uncorrupt and disinterested leader. His denial of tender feelings, or at least their displacement, permits him not only to stay at meetings and congresses when others have long since gone home to their families but also, and less trivially, to face exile or prison. And so forth.

Now the fascinating thing for me is that, in spite of its strong Puritan background, what I am calling revolutionary asceticism is conspicuously absent in the American Revolution. Hobsbawm is wrong when he says that no well-established organized revolutionary movement, to use his terms, is without a puritanism to which it succumbs. Unless I am badly mistaken, there is simply no important counterpart to a Robespierre or a Lenin, the prototypes par excellence of the revolutionary ascetic, in the American Revolution. Washington, for example, is no more a revolutionary ascetic than he is a charismatic personality.

Why is this so? The answer, I believe, confirms certain judgments about the American Revolution. To make my point, however, I must return briefly to my thesis about the revolutionary ascetic. It is my contention that the traits of traditional asceticism and displaced libido became increasingly funcional in the service of revolutionary activity with the following developments: (1) the emergence of revolution as a profession, i.e., a lifetime career, as exemplified first in the early 19th century by Blanqui and Buonarroti and later by Bakunin, Marx, Lenin, Castro, Mao Tse-tung, and so forth; (2) the achievement of modernization by means of a revolution, i.e., where private ascetic capitalism was insufficient and only a party or state form of Weber-like asceticism could take its place; and (3) the need for either antifeudal or colonial revolutions, where the desire for a new identity called for violent rejection of the past and a sharp break with former ties of loyalty. Where these conditions obtained, leaders who were revolutionary ascetics held high cards. The situation favored their kind of personality, and their kind of personality further shaped the situation.

This was not the case with the American Revolution. Although primarily of the colonial revolutionary type, in my view, it was not modernizing in intent, not rejecting of its own past, and not made by professional revolutionaries. Although it was a war of independence, it was not one of liberation of the type associated with colonial revolutions today, for America had never been conquered by a foreign power and culture. As Louis Hartz has argued, there was no feudal or ancient regime to be rejected, and as Wesley Frank Craven shows in *The Legend of the Founding Fathers,* the colonialists appealed to their own history as support for what they saw as a continued and legitimate assertion of right.[8] Thus there was no need—indeed, no room—for revolutionary ascetic leaders. Instead, the colonists had two models before them of what a leader should be like: one, from the Puritan tradition, of a Moses type who would lead his people through the difficulties and dangers of the wilderness, as Cotton Mather claimed John Winthrop had done at the beginning; and the other, from the Roman inspiration, of a Cincinnatus who combined military prowess with agrarian virtue. The composite is hardly the model of a modern revolutionary ascetic.

Why, however—to go on with the matter—with so strong a Puritan ethos in the country was there no Puritan army, no Cromwell? Part of the answer is that the American Revolution took place not in the 17th century but in an enlightened 18th century. Another part is that the Puritan ethos did not need revolutionary efforts to help it modernize the country, a process that was taking place under private auspices, by society rather than the state. True, the Puritan ethic was invoked, as Edmund S. Morgan has told us, in support of nonconsumption and nonimportation. Frugality was also seen as "renewing ancestral virtues" and as the basis of freedom and independence.[9] As Morgan also informs us, however, the austerity campaign was not supported by the very merchants whose ethos it was—but whose commercial interests paradoxically pulled them in another direction. So, too, the fear of corruption in Puritan provincial America, as Richard L. Bushman has described it in an earlier paper in this symposium series, might have been expected to produce revolutionary ascetic consequences. Certainly there was a residue of the fear that power would corrupt— reflected in the writings of James Madison, among others—but it led to restraints on leaders rather than to grants of greater power to incorruptibles such as Robespierre. In provincial America, as Bushman informs us, "There is precious little evidence that the legislature was corrupted in the towns where the deputies were chosen or in the capital where patronage was dispensed."[10] Only when, as in England, political corruption was seen by Americans as subverting liberty and not just serving avarice did it become a real psychological threat. Even then, however, it did not give birth to revolutionary ascetic leaders.

★   ★   ★

So far, we have been circling warily around the edges of the psychological dimension of leadership in the Revolution. Necessary as such preliminaries may be, it is time now to get closer to the center, even though the approach may involve tenuous assertions of a kind that make orthodox historians uncomfortable. As an outsider to American history, I am again surprised at how few existing psychohistorical studies there are. It is paradoxical that in the country most hospitable to Freudian psychoanalysis there are so few psychologically informed studies of its Revolutionary leaders; compare the number of works, say, on Adolf Hitler to those, say, on George Washington. At a period when such prominent leaders as James Otis, George III, and the earl of Chatham had ostentatious nervous breakdowns and fits of insanity, one might expect the psychological aspect of leadership to be highly visible. Nevertheless, although William Willcox has studied Sir Henry Clinton and the great Lewis Namier himself has tackled Charles Townshend, the Revolutionary leaders themselves have been largely exempt from treatment in psychohistorical terms. (The studies of Jefferson by Erik Erikson and Fawn Brodie promise to change this situation in at least one case.)

If we turn from individuals to groups, we find the pioneering work of John Demos. There is also one other recent work that I find most exciting: "The American Revolution: The Ideology and Psychology of National Liberation," by Edwin G. Burrows and Michael Wallace. It is a natural extension, it seems to me, of the ideological-idealist interpretation of the Revolution so brilliantly expounded by Bernard Bailyn, who, I might add, has done penetrating psychological profiles on Jefferson and John Adams.[11] As one of Bailyn's pupils, Gordon Wood, remarks, "We must . . . eventually dissolve the distinction between conscious and unconscious motives, between the Revolutionaries' stated intentions and their supposedly hidden needs and desires, a dissolution that involves somehow relating beliefs and ideas to the social world in which they operate."[12] This is almost a definition of psychohistory. I assume it is one reason why I am here. Whereas the first papers of this symposium were published under the title *The Development of a Revolutionary Mentality* and restricted to conscious motives and stated intentions, both the Burrows-Wallace book and my paper take into consideration the unconscious and supposedly hidden desires as well.

To further this investigation, I now propose to make some comments on the Burrows-Wallace study, as establishing the basic psychological context for Revolutionary leadership, and then briefly to look at George Washington in this light. The Burrows-Wallace theses can be simply put, though such a summary does not indicate the wealth of detail and subtlety of interpretation that they bring to their task. According to these authors, Revolutionary leaders were faced with the need to break former dependency ties—in short, to assert independence—while dissipating the anxiety of Americans that they were not yet fit or mature enough for such a break. This break was effected in the general context of a challenge to patriarchal authority in the English, and indeed the European, world, as symbolized in Locke's polemic against Filmer in the *First Treatise on Government*. Thus, one result is the surprising frequency with which the polemical literature on both sides was filled with allusions to father, mother, and sons (I might add that, not unexpectedly, allusions to daughters are notably absent), and their relations to one another. For Burrows and Wallace, these are collective symbols, not Oedipal images. In any case, England as a protective paternal and nurturant maternal image is rapidly perceived as changing to a threatening parent, wishing to kill its child. The child's response is a terrible sense of betrayal, leading to paranoid accusations of conspiracy and of being attacked first. At the end, Burrows and Wallace conclude that the real issue "appeared to be not so much economic grievances [such as "restrictions on colonial manufactures and arbitrary taxation of colonial commerce"] as symbols of humiliation and degradation." So provoked, the rebels were able to feel justified in the release of anger against the parental figure, eventually sanctioned by the Revolutionary ideology, which also "pointed it toward the ultimate goal of independence."[13] Thus in their conclusion they link their psychology with Bailyn's ideology—Bailyn himself had pointed ahead to this link when he described the ideology of the American Revolution as the "radical idealization and rationalization of the previous century and a half of American experience."[14]

Basically, I think Burrows and Wallace have the picture right. Let me therefore put a gloss on it, indicating where I hope to be extending and perhaps refining the analysis. What we have here, in fact, is the particular American version of the necessary break in ties of affection that we discussed earlier in terms of the revolutionary ascetic, only in this case the tie is with a father-mother image rather than with the past of a feudal or ancient regime or with a foreign cultural overlay. This peculiar American version of breaking affective ties befits the particular kind of colonial revolution that we have described it as being.

The first thing is to refine Burrows and Wallace's use of paternal and maternal images. They are really not interchangeable. As I read the numerous quotes, the father is the true authority figure; he is embodied in George III, who is "father" of the country and empire. When the father's authority is seen as unjustly exercised, the sons have a right to reject it. As "Sons of Liberty," they struggle with the father and become in turn "Founding Fathers" in their own right. And what a happy coincidence for the psychohistorian that George III gives way to another George as father of his country. In fact it is worth noting that the authority is pluralized, for there is not just one American father, as in most other, similar revolutions, but a number of them. The Founding Father, in reality, is a peer group.

Were there any demographic and family changes in 18th-century America that coincided with this psychological shift? It is here that the work of Demos, Greven, and others becomes so important. As Burrows and Wallace sum up the matter, patriarchal authority in the colonial American family was in a pronounced state of disintegration. Let me also remind you that by the early 19th century Tocqueville could assert that "as soon as the young American approaches manhood, the ties of filial obedience are relaxed day by day." Was this relaxation of authority the result of struggle? Tocqueville assures us otherwise. "It would be an error," he says, "to suppose that this is preceded by a domestic struggle in which the son has obtained by a sort of moral violence the liberty that his father refused him. The same habits, the same principles, which impel the one to assert his independence predispose the other to consider the use of that independence as an incontestable right."[15] In short, the fathers cannot deny to the sons the same right they had asserted for themselves.

Now if Tocqueville is right, Americans experienced a different development at the end of the 18th century from that which their peers in Europe were undergoing. There, father-son conflict raged in increasingly open and violent terms. What Tocqueville calls "a sort of moral violence" is later labeled by Freud as "an Oedipal conflict" and is obvious in Diderot's *Rameau's Nephew*, John Stuart Mill's "Mental Crisis," Turgenev's *Fathers and Sons*, and numerous other accounts, both fictional and true. Was America really exempt from such struggle? Did the American Revolution traumatically solve the problem once and for all, energized by a concurrent evolution (rather than revolution) in domestic relations, an evolution strengthened in the future? I do not know. Burrows and Wallace, in a footnote, mention Francis Hopkinson's *A Pretty Story*, published in Philadelphia in 1774, which tells of "sons contesting their parents' administration of the family properties," and also cite Freneau's poem "To the Americans."[16] Only a further search of the literature can tell us what the true state of affairs was in this area.

One thing we do know for sure: the "son" in this case, America, was growing lustily. Between 1700 and 1760, the population of America went from 223,000 whites and 28,000 blacks to 1,268,000 whites and 326,000 blacks. What is more to the point, if we can extrapolate from other data, actual sons (and daughters) were extremely numerous proportionately to the general population. Thus in France, for example, there were 64.9 youths aged 15–29 for every 100 persons 30 years and over in 1776. The proportion of young people dropped steadily from that point on: by 1870–71 there were 50.3 youths per 100 persons in the over-30 group and by 1964, only 38.0. We can assume a comparable profile for America. Figures for the 18th century are lacking, but in 1870–71 the corresponding U.S. ratio was 86.4 per 100, reflecting a massive immigration of predominantly young people, and by 1965 it had dropped to 45.4; thus, we have levels generally similar to those in France, though not over the exact same time period.[17] In any event, it seems clear that sons were relatively strong in numbers in America at the time of the Revolution.

Connected with this sense of strength was the feeling of also being "purer." Whereas English leadership and authority were increasingly perceived as sinking into corruption, enervating luxury, and indeed effeminacy, the American sons prided themselves on their purity, manliness, and virility—all seen to be interconnected. As soon as the king showed himself as exercising his withering authority "unjustly," the sons could turn against him as a tyrant to be fought with righteous anger. Even in the fight, however, psychologically the sons needed still to identify with the parental figure, and this they did by establishing the fact that they were merely reaffirming the rights of freeborn Englishmen. Thus, they rejected the image of the bad father and appealed to that of the good father, thereby mitigating any sense of guilt and sin they might feel at opposing patriarchal authority in the person of the king.

The image of the mother is much more complicated. The paternal king symbolizes authority, whereas maternal England, the mother country, symbolizes nurturance. This "tender mother," as James Otis called her, generously gave her breast to her young offspring. The images are frequently oral, with much talk of suckling. So too, the mother country is seen as protecting the sibling colonies from squabbling among themselves. The feelings aroused are obviously quite different from those connected with paternal authority. Then suddenly, just as the father's authority had been perceived as unjust, the mother's nurturance is seen as being taken away. If anything, the reaction is far more violent. For John Adams, the mother country had become like Lady Macbeth, capable of plucking her nipple from America's boneless gums and dashing the brains out. He used the image in "A Dissertation on the Canon and Feudal Law" of 1765 and was sufficiently impressed, or compelled, by it to use it again in a letter of 1818 to Hezekiah Niles, where he stated that when the colonies found Britain to be "a cruel Beldam, willing like Lady Macbeth, to 'dash their brains out,' it is no wonder their filial affections ceased and were changed into indignation and horror."[18] One feels an especially personal element in Adams' usage, but it was in tune with others of his time. The former "tender mother" is now seen by Richard Henry Lee, for example, as a "step-mother," an "oppressive step-dame."[19] Worse, she is also "an old abandoned prostitute," refined in the "arts of debauchery."[20] Such violent language makes one think of Freud's theories about the child's split of the maternal image into the pure, protective mother, devoid of sexual aspects, and the fallen, violated prostitute. America in the 1770's seems to have swung violently from the overidealized image to the other, negative one. Was the split deeply rooted in the American psyche of the time, waiting to be exploited?

In any case, the breaking of affective ties with both parental images was now complete. One consequence was that the sons had become "new men" in a "Novus Ordo." It is interesting, however, to compare Crèvecoeur's new man with, say, the new man of the 19th-century Russian revolutionist Chernyshevsky, whose novel *What is to be Done?* had such enormous influence on Lenin. Chernyshevsky's new man was hard, self-controlled, and devoid of natural human feelings—the perfect revolutionary ascetic. Crèvecoeur's new man, as we all know, was one "who acts upon new principles; he must therefore entertain new ideas, and form new opinions. From involuntary idleness, servile dependence, penury, and useless labor, he has passed to toils of a very different nature, rewarded by ample subsistence.—This is an American...."[21] In short, with independence came a renewal of nurturance—"ample subsistence"—but this time also independence from the mother.

Such new men are self-made men, and it is no accident that Flexner heads the very first section of his three-volume biography of Washington "A Self-Made Man."[22] There is an interesting confirmation of this attitude toward mothers in Erikson's essay "Reflections on the American Identity." There, discussing "Momism" and noting the existence of countless case histories of patients whose mothers were either cold and rejecting or hyperpossessive and overprotective—again the split—Erikson comments that "behind a fragmentary 'oedipus complex,' then, appears the deep-seated sense of having been abandoned and let down by the mother, which is the silent complaint behind schizoid withdrawal.... But wherever our methods permit us to look deeper, we find at the bottom of it all the conviction, the moral self-accusation, that it was *the child who abandoned the mother*, because he had been in such a hurry to become independent."[23] Erikson, of course, was not thinking of the American Revolution and the paternal-maternal images that concern us here. Yet, there is a kind of uncanny feeling provoked in us by the coincident views, suggesting that much of our national character was annealed at the time of the Revolution. For this process to occur, the original elements had already to be present, in a way I can only guess at. In any case, independence was asserted from the mother and her nurturance at that time, as the sons stood now as free men. As for the father, his authority was assimilated by the sons as a whole, who were basically able to identify with him by seeing their revolution as a reassertion of existing ancestral rights.

In all of this a price had to be paid. Let me address myself briefly to a few parts of the inheritance. One is the terrible sense of betrayal which gathers strength in the Revolutionary period and waxes as the "paranoid style" in American life, so well described by Richard Hofstadter and others. It is intimately connected with the belief in a "conspiracy," wherein all acts of the parent country, however innocent, are interpreted as being part of a plot. A caution is necessary here, however: conspiracy fears are part of almost all revolutions—one thinks of the French Revolution's "Great Fear"—and therefore one must try to sift out what is special about them in the American Revolution. I believe that the particularity of the American case lies in its connection with the sense of parental betrayal as we have outlined it.

From a psychological viewpoint, one may also look for evidences of fear of body loss or injury, as analyzed in the case of children, for example, by Melanie Klein. Thus, Dickinson characteristically speaks of the colonists as "torn from the body, to which we are united by religion, liberty, ... we must bleed at every vein."[24] In this area too, we shall seek evidences of a fear of "poisoning," for example, of the "body politic." One would also expect data in terms of what child psychologists call "separation anxiety," the fears manifested by a young child when the parent leaves him. These, however, are all recondite subjects, and one would have to be very careful in translating psychoanalytic concepts into true psychohistorical work.

The evidence is firmer on a second issue: the sense of being attacked first. The accusations are numerous that it is the father who has first taken up the cudgel against the child. I must call your attention here to a most interesting analysis of the "American military experience" by John Shy, in the Winter 1971 issue of the *Journal of Interdisciplinary History*.[25] His thesis is that against a background of 17th-century colonial anxiety, insecurity, and violence the Americans saw the Indians as striking first and unexpectedly. An outside observer, alas, sees the reality as being one of Americans' projecting their aggressive impulses—in fact, they are the true invaders—onto the Indians as a way of effacing the guilt they might otherwise feel in themselves. In any case, Shy sees the Americans as developing a characteristic style of dealing with such a threat: not by means of a specialized, professional army but rather through military potential in terms of the great mass of people. "With great strength," he tell us, "but weak defenses, the colonies experienced warfare less in terms of protection, of somehow insulating society against external violence (as was increasingly true of European warfare), than in terms of retribution, of retaliating against violence already committed."[26] This belief, or style, was confirmed by the French and Indian Wars, where the attack seemed to come now not so much from the Indians per se as from unsuspected European wars, erupting mysteriously on the American continent; the belief is made a hardened conviction by the events of the 1770's. Thereafter, as Shy shows, Americans interpreted all their future military experiences in terms of being innocent, passive people who were suddenly and unexpectedly attacked. Once again, I suspect, this general pattern is especially connected to the feelings associated with the break in affective ties with the "parent" country.

Overwhelmingly, in all of the issues we have looked at, the symbolism of father, mother, and son seems paramount. These are the inner springs underneath the conscious assertions of constitutional right, economic grievances, and ultimately independence. Whatever their roots in American family life and experience, however vaguely and tenuously they manifest themselves, the feelings attached to this symbolism provide the psychological context in which leadership must exert itself. The leader of 1776 had to be strong enough to break the ties of affection with the parent country and to inspire others with the confidence that they too could sustain the shock. He had to offer a trustworthy substitute for the old authority—the image of a son who had become a Founding Father. He had also to provide promise of nurturance which would take the place of that formerly provided by the mother country. He needed to assuage feelings of parricidal guilt by justifying the filial release of anger and resentment. He had to inspire confidence that, though unjustly and unexpectedly attacked, he would persevere until the unprepared military potential could be mobilized to overcome the enemy. Above all, he had to unify all these feelings into a new continental synthesis, expressed consciously in a new ideology and imaged forth for all to see in the person of a "new man": the American.

In 1776, no one man emerged to be "the leader." Instead, sons grew up in peer-group fashion to become Founding Fathers, a development certainly conformant with the existence of sibling colonies. Thus only detailed analyses of all the Founding Fathers could offer the evidence as to how each, out of the experiences of his own personal life, was able to contribute to the psychological synthesis of leadership in the American Revolution. Among them, however, there was one who was primus inter pares: George Washington. Above all the others, he symbolized the new "father of his country" who stood for unity of action against the authoritarian king and the no longer nurturant mother country. What fit of personal development and national need can we detect in his life history? Let us see if there are any hints that we can offer a future inquirer into this subject.

It must be said right off that any effort at an Eriksonian life history will confront major difficulties. In his studies of Luther and Gandhi, Erikson analyzed primarily religious figures who only secondarily became involved with political revolutions. In his terms, by having first solved their own identity problems, they were able to offer a solution to the identity crisis of large numbers of people and, in the process, to become "second fathers" to their followers. Now this sounds helpful to us in our study of the American Revolution. Whatever the Puritan aspect of America, however, it was within an Enlightenment context of nonreligious or even anti-religious belief that a leader such as Washington developed (though he was an Anglican by form). There was no crisis of faith, no challenge to au-thority in a religious guise. Thus, to provide salvation for an individual or a group was not one of the demands made on a potential leader. Instead, military endurance and continental unity were required. A better model for the study of Washington is therefore probably provided by Mustapha Kemal Pasha of Turkey, strange as it sounds, than by Luther or Gandhi.

The next difficulty is that Washington was simply not an introspective man. Though he left letters and diaries that now fill over 40 volumes, he revealed little of his personal feelings in them—indeed, as we shall see, a major component of his personality was coldness and reserve. Unlike Gandhi, he wrote no autobiography. Unlike Luther, he did not tabletalk with disciples. How are we to get inside this man? Is there all that much inside to be gotten at? There seems no identity crisis, no trauma to have lent drama to his inner development. Thus as Marcus Cunliffe suggests, "His personality baffles because it presents the mystery of no mystery."[27]

Yet he did have a personality. Consequently, out of his life experiences, let us draw not a life-historical sketch—an impossibility here, if not at any time—but four or five themes that relate to psychological dynamics operat-ing at large, which Burrows and Wallace have pointed us toward. The first theme we notice is the omnipresence of parental and sibling loss. It runs through Washington's whole family history. His father, Augustine, lost his own father at age three and then his mother at seven. George's mother, Mary, also lost her father at three and then her mother at 12. Hence, both grew up in the tutelage of stepparents or guardians. This, then, was George Washington's grandparental heritage, so to speak. George himself lost his father at age 11. Before this, a sibling—a half-sister—had died when he was three and another sister had died in infancy when he was about eight.

Now, to say that such family losses were characteristic of the times is merely to indicate how resonating would be George's personal experience (although we must also realize that, as a result, such loss would have a somewhat different quality from what it has today). The problem would still be one of how to deal with the death fears and wishes, the anxiety at separation—incidentally, the family uprooted itself three times before George was seven—and the mourning and melancholy occasioned by these removals. I suggest that we view the emotions aroused by this problem under the term *threat of abandonment.* For a child to counter such a threat, I believe, would mean generally having to learn early to deny close affective ties, to be willing to see them broken where they existed, and to mature early into feelings of independence.

Such traits in a mature Washington, as leader of his people, would correspond fittingly with the needs of the situation in the 1770's. A glimpse of this fact is what may have led Cunliffe to describe Washington as "a sort of splendid foundling at the head of a foundling nation."[28] In some ways, Washington had never known—or at least felt he had never known—a proper father. As Freeman tells us apropos of the death of George's father, "He had seen little of his father and in later life he was to remember only that his sire had been tall, fair of complexion, well proportioned and fond of children."[29] This paucity of memory—extraordinary if we remember that George was 11 years old when his father died—suggests a major blocking of feeling toward the father, allowing later disengagement from another parental image without undue rancor.

Our second theme is, alas, incipiently Oedipal. George's mother was 23 when she married his father, who was 37 at the time. In classic Freudian terms, little children often wonder how a young mother can be married to an almost grandfatherly type. Did young George so wonder? This would be especially likely, since a half-brother, Lawrence, aged 20, returned from school in England in 1737, when George would be at the ripe Oedipal age of 5. Freud himself had assumed that his own mother at 21 should more rightfully sleep with his half-brother of about 20 than with his "old" father of 41.

Somehow, however, I doubt if things worked so classically for young George. The evidence, of course, one way or another, is nonexistent. What we do know is that George dealt with whatever Oedipal feelings were present by regarding his half-brother, Lawrence, as a kind of second father. When the latter married within two months of Augustine's death, George made his half-brother's house his own second home, adding parental regard for Lawrence's father-in-law, William Fairfax, to that for his brother. In addition, he treated William Fairfax's son, another George, as an equal or less, though the young man was several years his senior. It was the future wife of George Fairfax, Sally Cary, with whom Washington was to fall deeply in love only a few years later, when she was 18 and he 16. It is difficult to believe that, in the realm of the unconscious, George Washington was completely untouched by the Oedipal aspects of this relationship. The whole subject, however, is far too tortuous and unclear to do anything more than note it as in some way a background for Washington's feelings about parental and sibling symbolism shaping British and colonial relations. Only in terms of the substitute father-figure, Lawrence, are we on sure grounds. By identifying with him rather than with his real father, George Washington came to shape his identity as a military man, the role in which he most obviously offered leadership to the American Revolution.

We must say one further word about George Washington's mother, Mary. All observers agree that she was a demanding and "majestic" woman. She opposed her son's military ambitions and appears not to have approved of his successes. In fact, she seems to have constantly depreciated his achievements. In psychological terms, one would expect real hurt to young George's self-esteem, and therefore a constant need to prove himself. Here, indeed, we may find the root of his driving ambition, noted by all who have written of him. His mother's lack of confirming love seems to have reaffirmed the need for self-reliance and the absence of strong affective ties we have postulated earlier as being laid down by what we called the threat of abandonment. Washington turned "cold." As one later observer commented in 1784, "I could never be on familiar terms with the General—a man so cold, so cautious"; another a few years later noted that "there seemed to me to skulk somewhat of a repulsive coldness . . . under a courteous demeanor."[30] Rejected by his mother, Washington avoided deep intimacy with others. Although he certainly did not become a misogynist—indeed, he married a widow with two children and always prized his domesticity—he did not marry for love. Able, however, to reject his own mother, he could also lead his fellow Americans into a war that rejected, and expelled from the ancestral house, the mother-country, England.

Our last theme concerns Washington's sense of betrayal at not being accepted at his true worth and given a correct rank in the regular British army. Having identified himself with Lawrence, who had held a regular commission, George nursed expectations of similar treatment. When his deeply held hopes were disappointed, Washington became bitterly resentful—it appeared that the British army was rejecting his military ambition, just as his mother was doing. Indeed, in the years 1753–58, one senses a touch of what many of his biographers describe as paranoiac suspicion in the young Washington, as he sought preferment by every route and seemed to imagine it blocked by plots and conspiracies against him. It was only in 1775, after what we can view as an unusual kind of Eriksonian "moratorium" of 17 years in which he came successfully to terms with himself, that Washington was able to return maturely and independently to his first ambition, with what momentous results we all know.

It is time for me to stop. My few brief remarks on Washington are not even the shadow of a life history. I hope they are suggestive, however, even if perhaps occasionally wrong in their specifics, of the sort of questions one might wish to ask about the personal lives of the leaders of the American Revolution. The next question, of course, would be: how do the themes of their life histories relate to the psychological themes sounded forth by large numbers of fellow colonists, in pamphlets and books, letters and diaries? In fact, it is in the conjunction of these two sets of inquiries that we shall find the best answer to the overall question: what is the psychological dimension of leadership in the American Revolution? Only thus shall we come to know the Founding Fathers in the deepest aspect of their great creative effort.

Notes

[1] Dankwart A. Rustow, "The Study of Elites. Who's Who, When and How," *World Politics* 18 (1966):690–717. Cf. Harold D. Lasswell, *Psychopathology and Politics* (New York: Viking Press, 1960) and Daniel Lerner, with the collaboration of Ithiel de Sola Pool and George K. Schueller, *The Nazi Elite,* Hoover Institute Studies, series B: Elite Studies, no. 3 (Stanford: Stanford University Press, 1951).

[2] After this paper was written, I became aware of James Kirby Martin's *Men in Rebellion: Higher Governmental Leaders and the Coming of the American Revolution* (New Brunswick, N.J.: Rutgers University Press, 1973), which does provide the kind of study I claimed was missing in the American field. Fortunately, Martin's own admission that he was filling a gap does vindicate my initial observation.

[3] Charles S. Sydnor, *American Revolutionaries in the Making* (New York: Free Press, 1965), p. 98. [Originally published as *Gentlemen Freeholders*]

[4] Seymour Martin Lipset, *The First New Nation* (Garden City, N.Y.: Doubleday & Co., 1967), p. 21.

[5] Henry T. Tuckerman, *Essays, Biographical and Critical* (Boston, 1857), quoted in Marcus Cunliffe, *George Washington, Man and Monument* (Boston: Little, Brown and Co., 1958), p. 223.

[6] E. J. Hobsbawm, in *New Society* (May 22, 1969).

[7] Sigmund Freud, *Group Psychology and the Analysis of the Ego,* in *The Standard Edition of the Complete Psychological Works,* trans. and ed. James Strachey, vol. 18 (London: Hogarth Press, 1955), pp. 123–24.

[8] Louis Hartz, *The Liberal Tradition in America* (New York: Harcourt, Brace & World, 1955); Wesley Frank Craven, *The Legend of the Founding Fathers* (New York: New York University Press, 1956).

[9] Edmund S. Morgan, "The Puritan Ethic and the Coming of the American Revolution," in Jack P. Greene, ed., *The Reinterpretation of the American Revolution, 1763–1789* (New York: Harper & Row, 1968), p. 241.

[10] Richard Bushman, "Corruption and Power in Provincial America," in Library of Congress Symposia on the America Revolution, 1st, 1972, *The Development of a Revolutionary Mentality* (Washington: Library of Congress, 1972), p. 72.

[11] John Demos, "Underlying Themes in the Witchcraft of Seventeenth-Century New England," *American Historical Review* 75 (1970):1311–26; Edwin G. Burrows and Michael Wallace, "The American Revolution: The Ideology and Psychology of National Liberation," *Perspectives in American History* 6 (1972):167–306; Bernard Bailyn, "Boyd's Jefferson: Notes for a Sketch," *New England Quarterly* 33 (1960):380–400, and "Butterfield's Adams: Notes for a Sketch," *William and Mary Quarterly,* 3d ser. 19 (1962):238–56; Cf. Bailyn's comments in "Common Sense," in Library of Congress Symposia on the American Revolution, 2d, 1973, *Fundamental Testaments of the American Revolution* (Washington: Library of Congress, 1973), p. 17.

[12] Gordon Wood, "Rhetoric and Reality in the American Revolution," *William and Mary Quarterly,* 3d ser. 23 (1966):3–32; reprinted in *Revolution; a Comparative Study,* ed. Lawrence Kaplan (New York: Random House, 1973), pp. 128–29.

[13] Burrows and Wallace, "American Revolution," pp. 209, 304.

[14] Bernard Bailyn, quoted in Greene, ed., *Reinterpretation of the American Revolution,* p. 55.

[15] Alexis de Tocqueville, *Democracy in America,* 2 vols. (New York: Colonial Press, 1900), 2:202.

[16] Burrows and Wallace, "American Revolution," p. 203.

[17] See Herbert Moller, "Youth as a Force in the Modern World," *Comparative Studies in Society and History* 10(1968):237–60.

[18] Quoted in Burrows and Wallace, "American Revolution," pp. 194, 292.

[19] Quoted in Merrill Jensen, *The Founding of a Nation* (New York: Oxford University Press, 1968), p. 199.

[20] Burrows and Wallace, "American Revolution," pp. 202, 213.

[21] Quoted in Jensen, *Founding of a Nation,* p. 12.

[22] James Thomas Flexner, *George Washington; the Forge of Experience (1732–1775)* (Boston: Little, Brown and Co., 1965), p. 7.

23 Erik H. Erikson, "Reflections on the American Identity," in *Childhood and Society,* 2d ed. (New York: W. W. Norton & Co., 1963), p. 296.

24 Quoted in Burrows and Wallace, "American Revolution," p. 290.

25 John Shy, "The American Military Experience: History and Learning," *Journal of Interdisciplinary History* 1 (1971):205–28.

26 Ibid., p. 213.

27 Cunliffe, *George Washington,* p. 185.

28 Ibid., p. 210.

29 Douglas Southall Freeman, *George Washington, a Biography,* 7 vols. (New York: Scribner, 1948–57), 1:71–72.

30 Cunliffe, *George Washington,* p. 189.

BRUCE MAZLISH taught briefly at the University of Maine, Columbia University, and the Massachusetts Institute of Technology before his appointment in 1953 as director of the American School in Madrid. He returned to M.I.T. in 1955, where he has served as professor of history since 1965 and as chairman of the History Section from 1965 to 1970.

Professor Mazlish holds B.A. (1944), M.A. (1947), and Ph.D. (1955) degrees from Columbia University. During World War II he served in the Infantry and the OSS.

His publications include *The Western Intellectual Tradition* (with J. Bronowski, 1960), *Psychoanalysis and History* (1963, 1971), *The Railroad and the Space Program; an Exploration in Historical Analogy* (1965), *The Riddle of History* (1966), *Revolution: A Reader* (with A. Kaledin and D. Ralston, 1971), and *In Search of Nixon; a Psychohistorical Inquiry* (1972). He is also editor of the series *Main Themes in Modern European History.* Professor Mazlish is a fellow of the American Academy of Arts and Sciences and, in 1972–73, was a visiting member of the Institute for Advanced Study. He is on the editorial boards of *History and Theory,* the *Journal of Interdisciplinary History,* and the *History of Childhood Quarterly.*

Library of Congress Publications
for the
Bicentennial of the American Revolution

The American Revolution: A Selected Reading List. 1968. 38 p. 50 cents. For sale by the Superintendent of Documents, U.S. Government Printing Office, Washington, D.C. 20402.

The Boston Massacre, 1770, engraved by Paul Revere. Facsim. $2. For sale by the Information Office, Library of Congress, Washington, D.C. 20540. Creating Independence, 1763–1789: Background Reading for Young People.

A Selected Annotated Bibliography. 1972. 62 p. $1.15. For sale by the Superintendent of Documents, U.S. Government Printing Office, Washington, D.C. 20402.

The Development of a Revolutionary Mentality. Papers presented at the first Library of Congress Symposium on the American Revolution. 1972. 158 p. $3.50. For sale by the Information Office, Library of Congress, Washington, D.C. 20540.

English Defenders of American Freedoms, 1774–1778: Six Pamphlets Attacking British Policy. 1972. 231 p. $4.75. For sale by the Superintendent of Documents, U.S. Government Printing Office, Washington, D.C. 20402.

Fundamental Testaments of the American Revolution. Papers presented at the second Library of Congress Symposium on the American Revolution. 1973. 120 p. $3.50. For sale by the Information Office, Library of Congress, Washington, D.C. 20540.

Periodical Literature on the American Revolution: Historical Research and Changing Interpretations, 1895–1970. 1971. 93 p. $1.30. For sale by the Superintendent of Documents, U.S. Government Printing Office, Washington, D.C. 20402.

To Set a Country Free. An account derived from the exhibition in the Library of Congress commemorating the 200th anniversary of American independence. 1975. 75 p. $4.50. For sale by the Information Office, Library of Congress, Washington, D.C. 20540.

Twelve Flags of the American Revolution. 1974. 13 p. $1.25. For sale by the Information Office, Library of Congress, Washington, D.C. 20540.

Two Rebuses from the American Revolution. Facsim. $2.50. For sale by the Information Office, Library of Congress, Washington, D.C. 20540.